HOW TO WRITE EDIT & PUBLISH YOUR MEMOIR

ADVICE FROM A BESTSELLING MEMOIRIST

BY

CAROLYN JOURDAN

WITH TIPS FROM

BOB TARTE * GEORGE HODGMAN

MARK GARRISON * JEREMY BLACHMAN

MARYANN FRY * C.A. WULFF

ISBN: 978-1-946299-08-6 (ebook)

ISBN: 978-1-946299-09-3 (print)

Dedication

I wrote this little primer because I get asked nearly every day, sometimes more than once a day, how to write a memoir.

We all have the same questions. And these questions reflect perfectly understandable concerns.

Here are my answers to the questions I get asked—and more importantly—to the questions I *don't* get asked.

I hope it helps you.

Contents

WRITING

Why Write a Memoir?

There are many possible reasons to write a memoir.

It helps to be clear in your own mind about your motivation for embarking on a memoir so you can be more efficient in your work. Be honest, at least with yourself, about what's motivating you.

Ask yourself: What's my point? What do I hope to achieve by writing a memoir?

Here are some reasons for writing a memoir:

1. To create a record of events for my family
2. To examine how I've lived my life with the benefit of hindsight
3. To share insights I've gained from enduring tough life experiences
4. To produce a work of literary merit using events from my own life as the subject matter
5. To give hope and uplift others by redeeming the unhappy events of my life and sharing the transformative skills I've gained from the mistakes I've made and problems I've faced
6. To get revenge on people who were mean to me
7. To share the misery I've endured
8. Other
9. All of the above

Types of Memoirs

There are different types of memoirs. The first two categories are broad, but it's important to be realistic with yourself (and especially with your potential readers) about the overall tone of your memoir.

Is it uplifting (Inspirational)?
Is it depressing (Misery Memoir, *aka* Misery Porn)?

It's okay, normal in fact, if your book contains a mix of happy and sad events, but you need to be clear about the overall feeling you intend to leave the reader with after reading your memoir.

Once you've decided on the overarching mood of your book, there are some finer distinctions to consider, for example:

- Historical
- Comedy
- Satire
- Exciting
- Scary
- Spiritual
- Exotic Setting
- Extraordinary Experiences
- Tragedy

Once you're clear about your emotional and factual trajectory, the writing process becomes *much* easier.

My Personal Take on Categories of Memoir

There are some other ways of categorizing memoirs, especially behind the scenes among memoirists. This is my take on them. Bound to offend. But I'm trying to be myself here and honest, for what it's worth.

Literary memoirs—unredeemed tragedy, written using a lot of big words for readers who like dark material and are highly likely to be depressive themselves. Most book critics fall into this category also—so it's a closed circle of writing and reading a very specific type of material that has labeled itself in a way that makes it sound superior to all other genres and tone. No other types of memoirs can ever break into this world.

When I was asking what the deal was with so-called *literature* my local librarian, an extremely well-read genius, told me, "*Literature* is just another genre. It's just a particular style. It's not a superior form of writing." I agree.

Snarky memoirs—think *Vanity Fair*, great setting and dialog and character, but always putting the knife into the characters at various points in the story. Always writing from an aerial, above-it-all, stance that gives the writer leave to judge even the most personal aspects of the subject's life. I adore *Vanity Fair*, but always feel simultaneously entertained and guilty when reading it.

Comic memoirs—in the same way that comedies rarely get Oscars, comic memoirs get treated as intellectually lightweight. I don't believe this is a valid point. I think it's purely a reflection of the fact that critics tend to come from the so-called *literary* world. There is such a thing as comic literature, in my opinion. For example, I was bowled over by the opening of the first *Dangerous Davies: The Last Detective* book by Leslie Thomas. I defy anyone to write a more gorgeous bit of prose than this:

This is the story of a man who became deeply concerned with the unsolved murder of a young girl, committed twenty-five years before.

He was a drunk, lost, laughed at and frequently baffled; poor attributes for a detective. But he was patient too, and dogged.

He was called Dangerous Davies (because he was said to be harmless) and was known in the London Police as The Last Detective *since he was never dispatched on any assignment unless it was very risky or there was no one else to send.*

Leslie Thomas was described as a person with no *edge*. I strive to remove the edginess in my own books. Keep this in mind. Are you writing edgy, gritty, sentimental, sweet? It's all good. But it ought to be a conscious, considered choice.

And you may discover that you naturally have a certain type of voice no matter what other sort of voice you're trying to achieve.

Misery memoirs—a long rant about bad things that happened to you. Unprocessed experience. Unredeemed hardship. These are very popular nowadays. I won't touch them. For me the entire purpose and process of writing a memoir is to make something good out of the difficult events of my life, to give them meaning that is uplifting and satisfying to me, and also to the reader.

To me, a memoir should involve taking the unpleasant experiences and processing them inside oneself with great effort over a long period of time and then, with the advantage of age and hindsight and a healthy religious or spiritual practice and transmuting them into hard-won wisdom. Then sharing that wisdom with others.

When a writer has processed and redeemed tragedy inside themselves, the reader can experience the catharsis with them. The memoir will leave them feeling elevated, ennobled, and satisfied.

If the obstacles faced by the protagonist remain unredeemed, the writer is dropping the reader on their head, leaving them with a giant buzzkill and to their own devices in finding a way out of a deep dark hole.

A lot of people buy these kinds of books, and they're a lot easier to write because you don't have to do any inner work to come up with material beyond the hideous facts and boring whining, but it's not for me. I prefer to struggle through a huge additional amount of effort inside myself so I have at least some modest amount of insight to share with the reader. Then I can live with myself more comfortably because what I'm putting out into the world is genuinely helpful.

At least this is what I tell myself. I hope I'm making good decisions.

Things to Know Before Starting

- Memoir writing is not like writing fiction.
- And it's not like writing other types of non-fiction.

These two basic facts are *crucial* to understand if you want to maintain your sanity while writing, editing, and publishing your memoir.

The fundamental ways that memoir differs from other genres will cause a lot more stress during the conceptualizing, writing, and editing process than other kinds of books. I remember telling my traditional publisher that their editorial process was like being operated on without an anesthetic. The editing and traditional publishing process felt like one of those nightmare scenarios where the anesthesiologist gives you the drug to paralyze you first, and then forgets to give you the other drug to numb the pain and make you unconscious.

WARNING: Memoir by its very nature tends to be extremely *personal*. Because it's about real events that happened to real people who are typically intimates of the writer if not the writer themselves, there's a great deal more emotional and psychological investment in the contents. Working with it is more fraught with trauma.

ANOTHER WARNING: Memoir is *subjective*. No matter how hard we try to be objective, the writing and editing of memoir is unavoidably subjective. No two people will have the same recollection of the facts, no two people will interpret the events the same way, and no two editors (or readers) will have the same response to the text.

A massive amount of *projection* occurs in the writing, editing, and reading of a memoir. There's no way around this. So be ready for this part of human nature to constantly be injecting an element of chaos into each stage of your work.

It's actually a character-building experience to endure the entire process and learn to cope with the vast array of things that people will say about you, your friends, your judgment, every aspect of your life, and everyone and everything you hold most dear.

I *loathe* character-building experiences. But by the end of the process you'll have a hide as thick as a rhinoceros. And that's a great thing to have. So go into this knowing that the insults and rabid attacks will only hurt for the first few years.

YET ANOTHER WARNING: Because of the special nature of memoir, the content of these first lessons may appear to wander, but there's a lot going on when you first embark on your adventure:

- Stress over trying to learning to write
- Stress over having to dredge up all sorts of highly emotional material and work with it over and over until you can render it properly in text
- Fear of exposure
- Your friends' and family's fear of exposure

That's a lot of heavy stuff at once. So we'll touch on a wide range of issues as we try to get a handle on our story and our process for rendering, editing, and publishing it.

I know a lot of memoirists and we're all different. We're different in *how* we write, *what* we write, and *why* we write. All I can tell you for certain is how *I* do it. I don't presume to think that my way is the right way.

The only reason I have the nerve to tell you about my way is that it has met with some success, so it's probably not the worst possible way for you to start.

Beginning Your Memoir

Start anywhere.

Getting those first few words down on paper is difficult, but it has to be done. If you can't get *any* words down onto paper, pause and reflect on this.

If there's one stumbling block every writer must overcome—this is it. You *must* be able to get words on a page *somehow*. If it helps, I can assure you that no one sits down and starts on Page 1 and writes a book manuscript straight through. That's just not the way it's done.

Probably the most helpful thing my literary agent ever told me was that you can never know what the first page of the book needs to be until you're finished. She said, "When you're finished you'll be able to see what the first page needs to be and be able to go back and write it so that the whole book will seem to inevitably follow from that."

And this turned out to be true in my case. The only time in my life I've ever had an experience hearing part of a manuscript dictated to me inside my head was several months after I finished the full first draft manuscript. I heard the first page clearly being read out to me inside my head like dictation. At the time I was sitting in a dark hospital reading room behind a radiologist friend watching him read x-rays. So I already had a pen a paper with me because I was taking notes about what he was doing and was able to jot down what I was hearing inside my head. It was a memory I was suddenly recalling where Daddy was showing me an x-ray and explaining what the picture meant. It was a perfect template for, a fractal of, everything that followed in my growing up in a doctor's office.

TRUE PATHETIC CONFESSION: I studied engineering in college. We didn't have to take much English and had little to no opportunity to practice writing prose. Everything was reduced to numbers and equations. The alphabet I worked with was mostly in Greek. I was such a hopeless case when I first started trying to write a memoir that when I finally got eight 1-page stories I can clearly remember holding the little sheaf of eight sheets of paper printed on 1-side only and looking at it in wonder, thinking, "Oh my God! I wrote a book!!"

I got unbelievably high from seeing my tiny book. Ecstatic. Then a few moments later, as I was admiring my little handful of pages, a voice in my head said, "When have you ever seen an eight-page book?"

Uh oh.

Well, we all have to start somewhere and this extremely modest start was indeed a start. And now thirty years later I have more than a dozen books and 7 top-10 in the USA best-sellers. So you never know.

Just. Start.

A Sentence a Day

Are you writing at least 1 sentence every day?

If you don't make some kind of a daily word quota and try hard reach that quota every day, you will never finish a book.

On his first book Charles Frazier aimed for 1 good sentence a day. And if you count the number of sentences in *Cold Mountain* like I did and you know the book took seven years to write you will see that this is literally what his output amounted to.

You can do 1 sentence a day.

But to do even 1 sentence you have to get over the fact that you don't know if you have any talent, or anything to say, or will ever be able to finish a book, because you can never know all that in advance. You have to go forward anyway. And you have to keep going forward anyway every single day no matter what.

Several of my favorite writers learned their craft by working for newspapers—for example, Dick Francis.

Dick Francis was the Queen Mother's steeplechase jockey who eventually became unable to maintain the strict dieting required of jockeys and had to find a new career. He got a job writing about racing for a newspaper. Later he produced a mega-bestselling horse racing mystery series.

Gregory McDonald who wrote the *Fletch* series also got started writing for a newspaper. And it's the same with a lot of other famous writers. They got good at writing by doing it every day.

There's a lesson there.

Talent

When I began to write *Heart in the Right Place* I had no writing talent whatsoever. In fact I had a form of dyslexia. Writing teachers told me time and again that I was writing backwards. I'd start a story with the punchline and then peter out after that, moving toward the beginning as I went down the page, but without having any consciousness about what I was doing.

I knew a good story when I heard it, but I couldn't write one down.

I was lucky and over the course of dating for 45+ years had three highly intelligent boyfriends who took some time to sit with me and show me my mistakes until I eventually learned to comprehend what they were saying.

For years after that my accommodation to my problem was that I wrote the text out the way I could write it—which was backwards—and then I just flipped it over 1 sentence at a time.

Eventually I learned to produce the manuscript in a more normal manner, but it took more than 20 years. And I still have to do the flipping, 1 sentence at a time, if I write a draft in a hurry.

Motivation

The only reason I ever wrote a book, the only reason I even started one—and the only reason I was ever able to finish one (after 14 years of intermittent struggle)—was because I lost my job and had no way to get another one. In a desperate moment brought on by hysteria I realized that the one thing I had to sell was the ridiculous story of the career decisions I'd made and what happened to me on account of them.

When I was trying to start my first book I realized that people hated lawyers and that I was a lawyer who'd had something terrible happen to them. It was my own fault of course, but I knew that people would enjoy watching a lawyer take a long hard fall. I'd had in the back of my mind, ever since reading James Herriot's *All Creatures Great and Small* that the everyday events in Daddy's office bore a remarkable similarity to that book.

And I admired the healing power of the sweet-natured, self-deprecating comedy in that book. I remember even today the way I felt after reading the last page and closing the book. I felt healthier and happier than before and like I was a better person. It thrilled me. So 35 years later my memoir became my version of *All Creatures Great and Small*—except with people and patients instead of pigs and poodles.

Stephen King wrote what most of my writer friends and I believe is the best book out there on writing. The title is *On Writing*.

What you learn in that book is the same thing that you'll learn from watching the film *8 Mile* which is that it takes a stupendous amount of motivation to produce excellent work in any art form, especially to generate that first work that will break you out of the pack. And the best way to get sufficient motivation is to have no way out of a hellish existence except to finish your book (or learn to rap really well).

If you have any alternative you may never be able to overcome the natural difficulty starting and finishing your first long form manuscript. At least this was true for me that first time (and also the second time). Now, after fourteen books, I know I can finish—eventually. But to be clear, both my first book and my second were written in utter desperation after losing jobs (ten years apart) and not being able to find another one.

This fear of not being able to complete a book is universal. Even Dean Koontz has to go stand in the library of his house some days and look at all the hundreds of books he's written in order to convince himself that the odds are good that he can finish the manuscript he's bogged down in.

So, no matter what problems you're going to face, most if not all professional writers have faced these same problems, too. The difference between a professional and everyone else is that the professionals soldier on despite their chronic worrying.

All this is to say, *You gotta get over yourself.*

Voice

Is the person telling the main story in your book funny, sad, whining, neutral, or arrogant?

When you've gotten over yourself and are finally trying to get started for real, a good way to do it is to try to think of one or more memoirs that really meant something to you.

You can look at those but you'll never be able to recreate any of them so, in some ways, it's a waste of time but I think everyone does it anyway just as a matter of basic orientation. What you're really trying to do, but you probably don't realize it at this point, is to discover your *voice*.

Voice is a mixture of word choice, the way you express yourself, your pervasive mood and tone, even your genre. And that has to be stabilized. Stabilizing a voice is easy for some, hard for others. It will happen over time. I'm particularly prone to producing text that will sound like it was written by someone with multiple personality disorder unless I stabilize my mood when I'm working.

For me my *voice* was an artificially learned, consciously stabilized narrator I think of as *her*. I am not that person, but I can pretend to be that person when I'm writing. I can pretend to be that person for hours, days, even twenty years on end. But it takes a *lot* of Diet Coke for me to do it.

You can't know your writing voice in advance. Just as you can't transcribe a standup comedy routine that was spoken aloud before a live audience and expect it to be as funny as the performance. Writing is a totally separate art form from speaking. The longer you write, the more you'll see that a book is a very special critter.

There's a difference in a spoken speech, an essay written to be read on NPR, dialogue for a movie, and text that's going to be read in a book.

Of course a book will have happy and sad and boring and exciting stuff all in there in various places. That's normal and good. What I'm talking about and what was hard for me was stabilizing an artificial version of me who was not writing one day in a sort of hyper mood, another day bored, another day depressed—so the underlying tone of the scenes was jumping around way more than it should.

I had to stabilize a voice for a *her* who was outside of me so I could write in *her* voice instead of whatever my mood happened to be on that day account of what was going on in my real life. It takes a while to write a book and you go through a lot of events in your outer life during that time and you don't want those ups and downs to make your manuscript uneven in a way that's coming from the outside—and not from the events in the story itself.

Organizing Your Material

There are several different preliminary organizational structures that you can try. They all work well. You'll probably need to use different ones at different stages as you progress with the manuscript. Use one until you exhaust it and then switch to another to generate more and different sorts of material.

Chronological

The most obvious way to organize a memoir is chronologically. But unless you have an unusually interesting sequence of events that may not be the best way to go. Writing a purely chronological narrative is a fantastic way to write a really boring book if you're not being careful.

WARNING: One of the brutally honest, but soul-destroying things you hear evil writing teachers say to budding memoirists is, "Just because it really happened doesn't mean anybody gives a shit." This, of course, is true. Just because something happened to you, doesn't mean anyone else will care (a sad fact of humanity) so always remember your job as a writer is to give them the type of material that will *make* them care. Tell them the parts of the story that will enable them to feel what you were feeling. Give the reader not just the dry external facts, but the emotional and psychological response to the facts.

Moments of Highest Emotion

Another way to start organizing your material is to start with the moments of highest emotion. You can use any kind of emotion. But it's gotta be strong.

I've written all of my books out of individually recollected moments of high emotional content, be it happiness, sadness, terror, frustration, … anything really. Those are the kinds of moments I'm most interested in, the moments I care about the most, and they are what motivates me the best.

I don't naturally have a linear or chronological structure inside my brain, though. Maybe you do, and maybe things can go a lot easier for you. I hope so.

When I'm writing about other people I make a list of questions about every sort of emotional situation I can think of and I take these questions with me on every interview I do. I've done it well over 100 times so far. I'll customize the questions slightly according to whether I'm gonna be talking to the Chief Bison Ranger at Yellowstone National Park or the head of pediatric neurosurgery at St. Jude's Hospital, but I'm actually looking for the same kinds of situations.

These are the kinds of things I ask (all in relation to the person's job): What's the most embarrassed you ever got? What's the scardest you ever were? When did you have absolutely no idea what to do? What's the funniest thing you ever saw? What's the dirtiest you ever got, the most exhausted, ….?

Although the interviewee may be a little nervous at first with these kinds of questions, I've never had a single person who didn't end up thinking the list was genius. I'm happy to share my lists with you if they'll help.

At the end of the next chapter are two of the actual lists I used to produce books—one for doctors and one for rangers.

Organizational Aids: Scrivener

Scrivener software is a wonderful organizational tool. There's a bit of a learning curve (not too steep if you're just using it for basic tasks like I do), but for Scrivener there are lots of excellent and economical online classes, free YouTube videos, and online tutorials you can Google up when you get stuck.

I might compose a draft in Microsoft Word (or rarely in Pages) but I'll transfer each bit of text into Scrivener where there's a sidebar *Table of Contents* that makes it really easy to see at a glance all the little bits you've accumulated so far and the sidebar makes it super easy to move the segments around into any order you want.

With Scrivener you don't have to do a lot of scrolling and copying and pasting like you would with a gigantic Word document.

Interviewing for Source Material

I've learned over the years that 90 minutes is about as long as most interviewees can go without becoming exhausted.

I've also learned to listen. Really listen.

It's amazing what happens when you're really listening to someone without judging them. We rarely ever do that. But when you do—and it's not easy—it's magic.

By doing nonjudgmental listening when you're interviewing someone you can create a deep bond with them that will last for the rest of your lives.

I've had two doctors I met only once, each for a brief interview, who called me years later from their deathbeds.

If for some reason you find that the interviewee is shy or having some other problem getting started speaking freely it helps tremendously if you inject some very short incident from your own life that will show them what you mean. But it's got to be really fast and really funny, or humiliating, or whatever the emotion is that you're trying to elicit.

Go ahead and mirror the emotion you're looking for and make yourself really vulnerable in front of the person you're interviewing. Humiliate yourself at least as much as you're asking them to.

All sorts of remarkable things can happen in these deep listening situations.

Here's one of the most amazing. It happened during an interview for *Medicine Men* and it was so astonishing I included it in the book:

"Hearing this story was especially moving because I'd waited a bit too long before going to see Dr. Adams. He'd had a stroke before I arrived. His mind was fine, but his speech was impaired, so he never spoke a word during the first hour or so of the interview. He'd just smile or nod as his wife told me their favorite family stories. I maintained eye contact with him the whole time, just as if he was speaking, but it was actually his wife who did all the talking.

Then, when we were nearly finished, she mentioned he'd been a doctor in World War II. She tried to tell me where in the Pacific he'd been stationed, but she'd forgotten the name of the place.

When she paused to think, the doctor said, "Torishima."

We were both startled to hear him speak. He repeated in a calm and steady voice, "It was Torishima. That means *Bird Island.*"

Then he told me this whole story himself in a clear voice.

[*Then in the book I relate the fabulous story he told.*]

The last line of his story was: 'I did that for over a year, then I got to go back home.'

As soon as he said the word *home* he stopped speaking. He never spoke again for the rest of my visit."

[Reading and writing this now is making me cry. It's moments like this that make all the tedious and agonizing work worthwhile.]

List of Doctor Questions

1. How did you get started?
2. How did you choose this field?
3. Most moving situation
4. Scariest situation
5. Craziest case
6. Most confusing moment
7. Most stressful situation
8. Most comical
9. Did you ever have to leave the room (couldn't keep a poker face)
10. Most tragic
11. Most touching
12. Most confusing
13. Most complicated case
14. Most unexpected
15. Most nervous
16. Most frightened
17. Most difficult procedure or situation
18. Hard to understand dialect or archaic medical terms
19. Poorest patient
20. Sickest patient
21. Cases you've never forgotten (most memorable)
22. Cases involving gunplay
23. Cases with no medicine or treatment available to help
24. Miracle cures
25. Supernatural or religious type events

List of Ranger Questions

1. Memorable moments with bears (or any critters)
2. Dirtiest you ever got
3. Coldest you ever got
4. Scardest you ever got
5. Most embarrassed as a ranger
6. Most humiliated as a ranger
7. Most angry (at animal or human)
8. Most confused, befuddled by an animal or human
9. Most lost
10. Most startled (by animal or human)
11. Most shocked (by animal or human)
12. Ever injured?
13. Ever trip or fall?
14. What would you never do again?
15. What's the hardest part of being a bear ranger?
16. What's the best part of being a bear ranger?
17. Did you ever get sick over something you saw?
18. What's the most uncomfortable situation you were in?
19. What's were the most difficult conditions you were ever in (cold, rainy, hot, windy, noisy, awkward position, crowded,….)?
20. What's the most important thing to know about bears in Yellowstone?
21. What else do you wish park visitors knew?
22. Best thing about Yellowstone? Worst thing? Wackiest thing?

War Memoir— Advice from Mark Garrison

Here's a list of a few things I wish I had done, along with some things that I did do from the outset.

1) I wish I had made a much more precise outline of what I wanted to say and how I wanted to say it. It would have given me a more accurate pathway to follow.

2) In the same vein, I would have kept asking myself if I was straying and detracting from my primary goals, or if I was supporting them, and giving meat to the story.

3) I wish I had placed less importance on what the length of the memoir was going to be. The length is less important than I thought. As a matter of fact, the inverse is usually true. An agent once told me that 70% of readers finish a book of 100 or less pages. A 200-page book is finished by 38% of readers, and if the book is 300 or more pages, it is finished by only 3% of readers. Those are sobering statistics!

The following principles are things that I feel are of extreme importance and that I tried to hold supreme:

1) Be as honest as you can be.

2) Do not embellish events.

3) If you are not sure about names, dates, etc., do some research.

4) Be authentic. If you're not honest and/or authentic it will be apparent to the astute reader.

5) Don't try to impress the reader with your astounding vocabulary. If the reader needs an unabridged dictionary to understand what you are saying, your book stands a much better chance of being a doorstop than a memorable read. The physicist, Steven Hawking once commented that for every formula that he put in his book he would lose fifty percent of his readers.

6) Understand that it is impossible to please everyone so don't even try. Stick to your mission.

7) A war memoir should reflect the way it actually happened. In combat description, don't water down the language because you're afraid you will offend someone, and you will offend someone. When hot lead is flying through the cockpit, you can't say, "MY! MY! Those bad men are trying to hurt me! My Goodness!" Use the language that was actually said, or it will obviously be phony and dishonest. It is history, remember?

8) Conversely, don't use profanity or hard language when it is not necessary or germane.

9) Carry a notepad so that you can jot down memories as they present themselves. If you don't have one, use a napkin or the back of your hand. Don't rely on being able to remember it later. As you write, memories will trigger a lot of other memories. You can count on it!

10) In a war memoir, know that some memories will be very painful to write about. Write about them, anyway! It's cathartic!

11) Realize that if you are going to edit the book yourself, after about the second time through, your own mistakes have a nasty habit of becoming invisible to your own eyes. Enlist the help of others that you trust. Remember, the more eyes the better.

Mark Garrison is the author of *Guts 'N Gunships: What it was Really Like to Fly Combat Helicopters in Vietnam.* His memoir is a *USA Today, Wall Street Journal*, and Amazon bestseller.

https://www.amazon.com/dp/B014TUIW7O/

Treating Your PTSD

You can use the same kinds of lists you use on other people to interview yourself. You can mentally interview yourself—but then you have to listen. To yourself.

This is where another magical process can take place. When you listen to yourself and write down what you hear, you're engaging in a deeply therapeutic process. The transference that can happen between you and your manuscript is profound. It's so deep you won't believe it until you experience it for yourself.

Psychiatrists and psychologists learned when trying to treat the PTSD of Vietnam veterans that if they would ask the veteran to write down what happened as closely as they felt safe doing, and by that they mean that you don't want to re-injure yourself by writing too explicitly about events that you can't handle.

The expert guideline is to write as close as you're comfortable to the actual events and then stop and set the manuscript aside. Then when you feel the time is right, you can go back and decide how you'd like to alter the manuscript.

You can gradually re-write your story so it gets closer and closer to the truth, or you can re-write it more in the direction of what could've been, what should've been.

Either way you get an unbelievably healing result, a miracle, from going back-and-forth between the manuscript and yourself—your brain and your heart. You're consciously deciding to dialog with yourself in the area between the objective and the subjective.

None of this material need ever be shown to anyone. You can share it if you wish, but it doesn't need to be shown to anyone else for you to be healed by the process.

Revving Up the Starter

There's no *right* or *wrong* way to approach writing a memoir. Everybody has to find their own way. Everyone's story is different. Certain common themes tend to emerge, but how you pick and choose the incidents that make up your life story and how you arrange them in your head so as to be able to get them down on paper is a very individual thing.

You can write about events that occurred over a long period of time, focus in on a brief interlude, or select several pivotal incidents and string them together.

You can move back and forth through the span of time in any way you wish. You can jump around some, but always be sure that the first few lines of every section make it clear what time and place you're talking about. (Unless you're writing an artsy book like *The Sound and the Fury* or *The Time Traveler's Wife*.)

My first literary agent was an editor for the Naval Institute Press at Annapolis. She read Tom Clancy's *Hunt for Red October* after it had been rejected everywhere. She told him something like, "If you'll put little captions before each section saying the local time, geographic location, and vessel the action is taking place on, then people can understand what's going on."

Tom did what she suggested and the Naval Institute Press published his book. Now virtually all thrillers rely on that captioning convention at the beginning of new sections. So keeping the reader clear about *where* and *when* he is and *who* he's with is really important.

Usually a book will start off with the strongest story and end with the second strongest bit (or vice versa). The best stuff usually goes first and last because that's what people tend to remember most. It's what needs to make a strong impression to engage their attention in the front and at the end leave them feeling they haven't wasted their life during the hours they spent reading your book.

When you're picking a place to start writing, depending on the level of PTSD you're dealing with, you can go to your strongest memory. Or, if that's too unpleasant or intimidating, you can start with something you feel safer talking about. And no matter what you think, nowadays we're *all* dealing with PTSD when we're well along in writing a memoir. If you don't think so watch the fireworks when you try to talk about or show it to any character you're writing about. (*Not* recommended.)

To start a story you write down what was said, what was done, how things looked, how they felt. You're writing a *scene*. Just like in a movie, but without any visual images or music to cue the reader's experience and understanding of what's going on. The loss of image and sound is *huge*. You have to make up for that in your writing. You have to be able to describe the scene well enough in text to give the reader all the information they need to follow the action and understand whatever point you're trying to make.

The loss of image and sound is why a written text of a standup comedy routine, or a radio show, or a film script, or a book—all dealing with the exact same scene—will necessarily have to employ significantly different words. A reader can't hear your tone of voice or see your gestures, facial expressions, or body language. They can't see the setting. Unless you help them.

This is a lot of stuff you have to give a reader with text. You don't wanna bog down in it though. How you deal with this interplay of telling too much and too little detail is called *pacing*. *The Da Vinci Code* is one of the most masterfully paced books ever. Every chapter ends on a page-turning cliff-hanger type of sentence. [His premise was blasphemous garbage as far as I'm concerned, but his pacing was a marvel.]

People will tend to overwrite some types of information and underwrite others. For example, I was born with some significant eye problems and as a result I'm mostly sound-based in my daily life. Sometimes during the day I'll find myself walking around inside my house with my eyes closed. I just don't use my eyes to the same extent that most people do.

My use of visual information is so odd a friend of mine who's blind once said to me, "Why aren't you looking at me when you're talking to me?"

He had some scars on his face from the explosion that had blinded him and he wondered if that was causing me distress. I explained that his scars were not putting me off. The problem was that I was shy and hesitated to make eye contact with anyone because my eyes weren't straight and I didn't want to see the awkward double takes as people tried to figure out which eye was looking at them. It was a habit left over from childhood on account of being called cruel names for having the wandering eye.

My friend told me I had more *blindisms* than he did. He said blind people were taught to look toward people's faces when they were talking to them. I said, "It's a lot easier to do that if you can't actually see the people!"

All this is my way of explaining that I tend to write mostly in dialog if I don't watch out. I have to go back and put in the visual description later. That's okay. You write down whatever you're registering and then go back during the editing process and add the missing information.

FUN FACT: Each of the strongest moments in a book will attract both lovers and haters. It's a fascinating phenomenon. *Medicine Men*, my first independently published book (indie, vanity, whatever you wanna call it—I call it "the poorly proofread .doc I uploaded directly to Amazon with 1-click after paying $19 for the cover image").

That book was rejected by three agents, my publisher at the time, and thirteen other publishers. It was said to be too short, too religious, too quirky … too everything.

I was truly desperate at the time. I'd lost my job and health insurance at age 58, had never married, and had just built a new house. So I published the little book despite *massive* rejection by well-regarded professionals all over the USA because I believed the material was wonderful and meaningful and uplifting. I wanted it to get out into the world. (Just like I want this little primer to get out into the world and help as many people as possible.)

Even more desperately than I wanted to make a living, I wanted to inject my two cents worth into the raging debate about health care. But because I believed all those publishing professionals had to be *sorta* right, I gave the book away for free.

Imagine my surprise when in 48 hours later it was #1 on Amazon. That day more copies of that book were going out to readers than any other book on the face of the earth. Literally. Hmmmmm. I felt God was speaking to me. In fact I felt that God was shouting at me. He was shouting, "Yes!"

Now there are 250,000 copies of *Medicine Men* out in the world and I've been paid for a lot of them. It's on national lists of best books and was voted one of the best healthcare books *ever* by Physicians Weekly.

Since then I've met several writers who are currently making half a million dollars a month or more on Amazon by indie publishing work that was savagely rejected by their agents and multiple publishers. They have much worse stories than mine. Appalling stories.

I suggest you always remember that. I know I will.

In this very important sense, you already know as much about the book business as you need to know. You know what *you* like to read. And if *you* like it, I promise you a lot of other people will, too. On Amazon you can find your people—your micro-niche. And doing well in a global micro-niche is plenty good enough.

Sorry, that was a necessary digression before making the point that every story in *Medicine Men* is really *strong*. The stories are short but they make a strong emotional impact. To me, they're like a drug. I get high off them. I knew they weren't for everyone, but by doing that book, I learned to trust myself, to believe in my own taste, at least for the quirky micro-niche genre that I was inventing.

I am now totally comfortable, even militant, about being myself. My writing is not for everyone.

But a fascinating aspect of quirky material is that when you have a really strong *bit* as I refer to them (scene, story, 1-liner, chunk of text) you'll hear from people who love it and people who hate it. Every single story in *Medicine Men* has people who adore it and people who insisted that it had to be removed before publication. Even the 1-liners.

I was told countless times that nobody wanted to buy a book with a 1-liner taking up an entire page. I didn't agree and only because I was literally hysterical at the time I published the book *my* way. And BAM!

So when people tell you: *This is the greatest story ever.* Or *You can't put this in there. You've gotta take this out.* Say to yourself, "Hmmmm."

Listen to what people say. They might be right. But they might be wrong.

Building Momentum

My method for starting a memoir is to make a list of the strongest memories that come to mind. You can work on this list over time and add things as you think of them. I find it easiest to start with stories that have a really strong emotional content. And that's what you want in your book—heart—emotion.

Personally, I start with the funniest stuff and work on those bits for a while to build some momentum. Other people might wanna start with the saddest or most stressful memories. Or you could start by making notes about favorite family stories you've heard told over and over. There's no right or wrong place to start. Start anywhere.

Starting at all is the hardest part. Just start somewhere.

Whatever you decide to start with, jot down some notes about of the highlights of the particular situation. Nothing fancy. Bestselling authors have been known to jot scene notes or outline ideas or theme concepts on McDonald's napkins (or napkins from Wendy's, Burger King, Arby's, Hardees, Krystal, KFC, Starbucks,….).

If napkins don't appeal to you, buy yourself some kind of notepad or notebook or ultra-small computer or use your phone to jot things down. Keep your notebook or device with you and write your ideas down as they pop into your head. I use any and all methods to make notes to myself. Sometimes I write in longhand, mostly I type into a computer, on rare occasions I will dictate into Pages using the excellent voice recognition software that come with all Macs.

Everybody has different neural pathways that will work best for them and which they can train gradually to make it easier and easier to produce text. Anything that works is great.

You can try to write a sentence or two about what you hope to say—your overall point, for example. You can scribble a very simple outline of your main character's Dreaded Narrative Arc (we'll talk more about this later). It's really important to try to figure out what's going to change inside your main character over time. What's gonna happen to them that's gonna to cause them to change?

If you keep making these sorts of notes and thinking about these types of questions you'll be able to refine your ideas over time. You'll gradually hone in on what you mean to say and discover how to say it more clearly.

Refining Your Concept

Nonfiction

There's a difference in conceptualizing a nonfiction project where you say to yourself:

- Here are the basic facts I have to work with.
- Which of these facts do I want to include, which ones do I want to leave out?
- What is my goal in writing this book?
- What is it that I want to say?

Nowadays the options for publishing are *waaaaaaay* broader than they used to be. There's enormous flexibility in length and topic and genre, especially with ebooks. That's a wonderful development (that's still evolving on a daily basis).

Very short books are now not only possible, but they are common. You can sell a 1-page book on Amazon. Ebook publishing costs can be nearly zero. You need not spend more than $400 for a professional looking book, and you can get a professional result for much less in many cases.

If you have a dynamite list for some common topic like *What to Pack for a Family Vacation at Disneyworld*, or *How to Do Your Own Home Inspection*, or whatever your expertise, you can write it up and share it worldwide any time you want.

This book is itself an outgrowth of the Facebook Group *Memoirists* that I created as an act of service to the world for my 63rd birthday. A side benefit was that I'd have a document I could send to the various strangers who contact me nearly every day, sometimes more than one of them a day, to ask me how to write a memoir.

I genuinely want to help everyone. I want to tell them what I've learned and save them as many hard knocks as I can. This primer will do that and also save me a lot of typing in email and Facebook Instant Messages. And it only took me 10 years to realize it!

Fiction

With a fiction project there are infinite possibilities limited only by your imagination, morals, and knowledge. Again, you have to find a concept you care about enough to stick it out and keep up the work of writing it.

Life circumstances forced me to learn to write by working on a nonfiction project, a memoir, so now I'm sorta stuck with that methodology. Even when I'm writing fiction I start from a base of facts I've gathered about some topic that I find really interesting. Then I develop a plot around that constellation of facts. Some of the topics I've used are antibiotics that can cross the blood-brain barrier, medieval French architecture, and some extremely unusual effects of testosterone.

The factor that makes a book appealing to me as a reader is *setting*. Most people read for character or plot, but I mostly want to learn about a place or a culture I'm unfamiliar with. So, when I write, I always try to include my own geographic and cultural details. Some quirky topics I always include are redneck life as I know it and live it and villains I've had the opportunity to experience as being a mixture of both good and bad. To make my books engaging, I try to use details from any obscure aspect of my real life.

An amusing thing about all this (that I never saw coming but have enjoyed in retrospect), is that I've made a decent living by writing about the very same things people criticized me for when I lived in the big city and held some important jobs—my hillbilly accent and my Appalachian manners.

I accidentally stumbled across a way to take the things that had been problematic in my life, like my career disasters and reviled ethnicity, repackage them, and sell them back to the same people who'd discriminated against me.

So anything quirky about you should be highlighted in your work. Distinctive is good.

Testing Your Concept

Dean Koontz says he still has to start a book and try to write it with his preliminary concept before he can determine if the book "will write."

I've stumbled over this problem, too (on a much smaller scale than Dean Koontz, of course). Sometimes you'll get pretty far along in a manuscript and lose momentum and give up. Most books die this way. Nearly all of them in fact.

You have to have a strong enough idea to motivate yourself for long enough to complete the project. You have to have an idea that you care enough about to work on it day after day. Most of the writers I know will toss around a lot of ideas in their heads but then they'll have some life circumstance that basically forced them to complete a book—any book. Do it and do it now.

For me and many others the crucial motivating factor in finishing a book was the loss of a job. My first two books each came after losing a job and having no realistic prospect for getting another one.

Daddy's retirement resulted in *Heart in the Right Place* and *Medicine Men* came after losing my job at the Great Smoky Mountains National Park.

Poverty is a fantastic motivator for writers, especially if there are no alternative sources of income available.

High Concepts

Books sell easier if they are created around a *high concept*.

A *high concept* is when a plot and characters are so simple and so immediately recognizable that the book can be summarized in 1 sentence or less. Preferably in a single phrase like the descriptions you see on movie posters.

Here's an example from a long list at http://www.filmdaily.tv/logline/top-box-office-logline-examples

The Godfather: The aging patriarch of an organized crime dynasty transfers control of his clandestine empire to his reluctant son.

I was very lucky and the story for my first book naturally had a *high concept*. In fact it had several of them: Riches to Rags, Arrogant Attorney Takes a Long Hard Fall, and Going Home, for example.

Or for the more detailed version of the high concept: *Heart in the Right Place* is the true story of a spoiled, high-powered Senate lawyer who gives up a glamorous life in Washington and comes back home to the Smoky Mountains to work as an inept receptionist in her father's rural medical office.

These quick summaries are also called *tag lines*, *log lines*, or *elevator pitches* (because if an agent is trapped in an elevator with you, you can pitch your book before they reach the next floor and the doors open again allowing them to escape).

What's a Story?

One of the years I was totally desperate while working on *Heart in the Right Place* I drove out to the University of Iowa Summer Writers Workshop (twice in one summer). This school is famous for teaching writers to write.

At the beginning of the first assembly on the morning of the first day a guy came out and said, "There are two things we cannot teach you: what's a story, and how to finish a project. Unfortunately, experience tells us that a lot of you will have one or both of these problems."

I'm an optimistic person, so I wanna try to do better than the world famous workshop by demonstrating what is a *story*.

Imagine an iconic image for the film *King Kong*, for example. You see a giant gorilla holding Fay Wray in one hand and the antenna atop the Empire State building in the other. Fighter pilots in biplanes are buzzing around him. New York City is in the background.

Instantly you understand that:

- Fay Wray has a serious easily understandable problem.
- King Kong has a serious easily understandable problem.
- The pilots have serious easily understandable problem.
- The setting is iconic and perfectly described.

This is a story.

It's also a *high concept*, i.e., the story is easy to grasp.

A story is an interesting character in a bind who suffers through a series of events while trying to extricate himself.

What's a Dramatic Arc?

A book is, roughly, a series of events in a 3-act structure.

This means there are sections of the book that are identifiable to a reader as a beginning, a middle, and an end.

If you don't have a text that has these three sections in this same order that the reader can sense as they are reading, your book is less likely to be coherent and satisfying to a reader.

We will explore this *arc* in more detail soon.

What's a Book?

A book about your life, a memoir, is composed of a series of fractals—each of which has a 3-act structure. A *book* is like a series of nesting boxes containing bits of text, *stories*, that are written in 3-act structures.

The narrative arc is the biggest box. Inside it are three medium-sized boxes for Acts 1, 2, and 3.

Each of the medium-sized boxes contains the stories in that particular Act.

The 3-Act Structure

Our current culture prefers a narrative to be told in a 3-act structure:

- Act 1 where the characters are introduced and their normal life is described
- Act 2 where the characters get into a conflict of some sort and their lives get majorly disrupted, and
- Act 3 where the conflict is resolved either by death or fast thinking or simply enduring a lot of pain and suffering that finally ends and all or most of the loose ends in the narrative are tied up.

Needless to say, most people don't experience their life in a 3-act structure. It's experienced from day to day as a bit of a jumble that we're constant trying to make sense of.

Writing a memoir will help you make sense of yours.

The Dreaded Narrative Arc

Most memoirs nowadays will not sell to a traditional publisher unless the main character has what is called a narrative arc. My friends and I call this The Dreaded Narrative Arc.

It means that a memoir has to be organized around a main character who grows and changes, becomes sadder but wiser, over the course of the book. The protagonist will face challenges that result in hard won wisdom and insight.

If you're writing nonfiction this mandate can present a crushing burden because at the time the events were taking place you didn't have the benefit of hindsight, so you didn't know where you were in the supposedly 3-act structure of your life. You were always present in your own mind as now this happening, now this is happening, and now…..

Commercial memoirs are generally crowbarred into a sort of John Boy Walton voice over to explain the significance of events you had no idea were going to add up to a *story*.

If you don't understand what I'm talking about, don't worry. It will become obvious when you get into the writing. When this happens let me know and I'll cry with you.

Let me try to say this another way. You know the stunning opening line of *David Copperfield?*

> Whether I shall turn out to be the hero of my own life,
> or whether that station will be held by anybody else,
> these pages must show.

This is a very real problem.

In real time, nobody ever knows whether they're going to be the hero of their own life. You can hope it works out to be the case in 70 years or so. But you don't *know*.

So to write a commercial memoir, you have to apply hindsight to the events of your life *so far* and formulate a structure that addresses this Copperfield conundrum.

If you're successful in concocting linear meaning from the random-seeming jumble of events that make up your life the memoir is satisfying. If not, it's disjointed, boring, and you'll never get an agent or a publisher (if you happen to want one. BIG WARNING: it's not what it's cracked up to be).

Early Drafts

Early drafts of a memoir, or any book, are generally awful, so don't worry about that.

The biggest problem in writing books is that writing is not easy to make yourself do. You have to sit down and focus your mind. I *hate* that. I'd much rather read or watch TV or drive around or do *anything* but sit still and focused.

A café is often a fantastic solution to this problem. There's food, drink, restrooms, and enough going on around you that you can feel like you're not actually alone and focusing.

They closed the last one of these I know about in Knoxville. Agony for me. Now I write in my car. I park in safe and reasonably interesting places and type on a laptop. That works pretty good for me. It's mostly a matter of training yourself to practice whatever routine works for you.

Every day, every day, every day.

Can't and Won't

People who *won't* write are a million times more common than people who *can't* write.

People who *can't* write usually have one of two main issues which are easily fixable.

Type 1: Can't

First are the ones whose book drafts read like an appointment calendar.

There will be a long series of *stories* that look like this:
"At 3:45 p.m. on June 4, 1986 I __(fill in the blank)__."

A few of those sorts of entries go a long way toward rendering a reader unconscious from boredom. Feeling, humanity, is missing.

Type 2 : Can't

Second are the people who can't conform to a 3-act structure.

There's no goal, no conflict, no struggle in the text.

Again, that's boring. The underlying material might be fantastic, these people often know a lot of wonderful stuff, but they render it as if it's just a slide show with no unifying narrative tension.

Travelogues or guide books or bad documentary films can be like this.

Writing a Memoir—
Advice from George Hodgman

I don't have a huge amount of advice except for the usual (regular writing time) but I have a few tips.

1. When you start to write, fire up the machine, be aware that it's on and that, if you pay attention during the times you are not writing to everything you see and hear, you can not only become more attuned to what constitutes bad dialogue and good dialogue but can also really gather a lot of detail. Listen for the sentences and comments and tones and accents etc. that can inform a scene but also inspire one. You are writing all the time. Remember that when you are away from the computer. Keep a pad or use your phone to email yourself. Get conscious about watching and listening.

2. At the end of each writing period or day make sure that you leave with a firm idea of what will start out the next day. Make sure, to avoid Blank Page Syndrome, that you know the first specific chore to begin your writing time so that you can hit the ground running. Make sure it's doable and something that can get you into the session.

3. What seems funny or necessary at the time, something worth risking someone else's feelings, something written at another's expense may seem vital on the day it is written but will embarrass you more than the subject on the day the book comes out and, well, for the rest of your existence. ALWAYS ERR ON THE SIDE OF GENEROSITY. Your subject may have motivations you cannot possibly know or understand.

4. Truth is always more complex than anything you "make better."

5. Go to an editor or other reader with very specific questions. An editor has no way of knowing what you have already tried and found unsuccessful. They may try to take you back over what you have rejected. Control the editing session by asking very specifically and concretely about the places where you have doubts or concerns: "Does this work?"; "Is this funny?"; whatever. Get your questions ready for an editor, don't wait for them and remember that general questions and responses usually get you nowhere. Editing is not a book report. You have to narrow down what you want an opinion about.

One last thing: if you can afford it hire a freelancer to do the responses to the copy editor. You'll be too tired of it to see stuff by then.

George Hodgman is the author of the bestselling *Bettyville: A Memoir*, a New York Times best-seller and a Finalist for the National Book Critics Circle Award. *Bettyville* is the hilarious and touching story of a cultured gay man leaving New York City to care for his aging mother in Paris, Missouri.

https://www.amazon.com/dp/0143107887/

What Makes a Book Bad?

Emotion

If you don't laugh and cry when you're writing and editing the book, it won't make anyone else laugh or cry when they're reading it either.

Some people write with too much emotion and too little plot (soap opera), but others have the opposite problem (dry recitation of facts with no humanity).

For years of working on *Heart in the Right Place* I worked only on the happy, funny stories. After about a decade of that I realized that being happy all the time wasn't a realistic depiction of a family doctor's office and I slowly, very reluctantly, started adding in the sad, and then the tragic, material. Although these sorts of incidents were extremely unpleasant for me to work with over and over, I soldiered on.

I was astonished at how the new material with different sorts of emotional content gave depth and meaning to the rest of the book.

It was terribly difficult for me to write the downer stories. Hideous. But I did it because it had to be there for the reader to experience the reality of family medical work. And developing the internal wherewithal to create this type of material was important to my personal development. It helped me move more toward a more balanced temperament.

Ugh. I hate it when I have to learn and grow as a human being. Agony.

You may find as you write more and more stories that they're all tending to be in the same mood and tone. If so, you need to think about that. It's probably better if the stories are arranged in wavelike sequences something along the lines of happy, neutral, sad, neutral, happy…. You repeat this sequence with a neutral story before and after each happy and sad story a bunch of times until the book is over.

I always end up having to make a chart that depicts just these repeating emotional tone arcs for every one of my books. I use little post-its for each story and place them on a 3-part folding cardboard poster from office supply stores. I've posted pictures of these charts on my Facebook pages.

It's not good to have a book that is one-third happy, one-third neutral, and one-third sad with huge chunks of each sitting right next to each other. (See the discussion about temperament below for more about this)

Action

To make an engaging book you need at least one main character who wants something (anything) and is having trouble getting it. His pursuit or avoidance of obstacles will create the main action in the book.

Books are boring if there's not some sort of struggle going on—physical, emotional, psychological. It can be anything.

The reason you need this is that a person's character is revealed by the choices they make. You have to include in your book the tough choices you've faced and what you decided to do, and why. That's the basic content of a memoir.

You can also add what you think of your decisions in hindsight. To the extent that your life struggles made you wiser, you should share that. The reader can benefit from your life lessons.

People who read biographies and memoirs tend to read a *lot* of them. These readers are interested in life experiences they will likely never get to have. They want to gain insight from people who've faced a broad range of situations. So if you're going to bother to write a memoir, you should share what you've learned about the world and life.

To write a *good* memoir you have to paint a coherent and moving word-picture of the events that shaped your new sadder-but-wiser persona.

The Dreaded Narrative Arc

If the main character doesn't grow and change over the course of the book (be a different sort of person at the end of the book than they were at the start) that's considered a bad, boring, pointless story—or a cautionary tale (a story about a person who never learned from their mistakes or developed any wisdom from life). Either way, the reader will feel disappointed.

Taste and Temperament of Writer and Reader

Why do you read what you read? Why do you like what you like?

Most people like to read material that is in a genre and tone that matches their temperament and reflects their own adaptive behaviors to the world. They read in order to confirm their world view. Most people do not like to read books that are written by someone whose temperament is uncomfortably different from their own, and/or whose adaptive behaviors to life's challenges are uncomfortably different from their own.

Every person has a temperament, a soul stance, that reflects their internal wiring. There are four basic temperament types. Each of these types have certain easily recognizable characteristics and they tend to have predictable adaptive behaviors to life circumstances. Most people aren't a pure type, but they'll notice strong tendencies if they're self-reflective.

We *like* genres that confirm our habitual soul state. We tend to *dislike* genres that conflict harshly with our habitual moods and responses to life. If we have the inner psychological tools to tolerate, to cope with, to *handle*, soul states that differ from our own, we can enjoy a wider variety of genres. If we don't have these skills we might feel afraid or unsettled or even angry when reading outside our comfort zone.

For example, I am highly sanguine and am unable to tolerate depressive material. My most obvious adaptive behavior to stressful conditions in life is to deflect upward into humor. In a work written by a depressive I feel like I am trapped and drowning. I panic and feel like I *have* to get away or I'll die.

Depressive writing makes me feel like Tom Hanks in *Castaway* when his Fed Ex airplane is crashing and sinking into the ocean. I will literally see flashes of that scene in my mind and it's my signal to cut myself loose. https://www.youtube.com/watch?v=HLi_w5rCH1I

That's just me. It says nothing about anything else. I cannot *enjoy* depressive work. Hundreds of millions of differently configured personalities can appreciate it very much indeed. For example, ten minutes of Dave Sedaris on audio talking about being an elf made me have suicidal thoughts. For real. I can admire his intelligence and wit, but he's too dark for me. I don't wanna to go there with him.

I'm a James Herriot, Leslie Thomas' *Dangerous Davies*, *Pink Panther* and *Logan Lucky* films, *Gentleman from Moscow* kinda person.

It would be great if reviewers were more conscious about this and could differentiate between books that were of a genre that they couldn't appreciate, and those that were actually *bad* or poorly written.

Which direction do you deflect in when something bad happens?

1. throw up your hands, sit on the couch with a bag of cookies, and try to forget about it (phlegmatic)
2. hope for the best, try to stay positive, leap in without thinking, and cheer everyone up (sanguine)
3. assess the situation, decide on a plan of action, and immediately start directing the repair efforts (choleric)
4. feel great compassion about the situation, want to help, feel sluggish in your responses (depressive)

Again, people with certain temperaments and adaptive behaviors will have varying tolerances to memoirs written by people with different temperaments and adaptive behaviors. For example, to a sanguine person, depressive material can feel like poison. Perhaps the opposite is also true. I don't know.

SIDE NOTE: This is why most comedians will tell you that you can't *teach* comedy. That's because comedy is a worldview, a soul stance. It's who you are (or aren't). Sanguine people don't have to *try* to write comedy or *learn* to write comedy, it's what they *are*. It's inherent to their nature. They can't help it. It's just what comes out.

But it doesn't mean they don't know what's going on. Comedy gets judged as intellectually or artistically *lightweight* (both in books and film) but that's a biased opinion (in my biased opinion). The genre is no less worthy than tragedy. It's just different. There are good and bad comedy books and good and bad tragedy books.

One writer I greatly admire, Alexander McCall Smith, is a bit of a switch-hitter in his writing. This ability is a rarity.

He has a huge body of work, but his breakout hit was the *No. 1 Ladies' Detective Agency* cozy mystery series set in Botswana. The 1st book in the series was much darker than all the rest that followed but in these books he captures the generous, positive, and gently comedic soul mood of an admirable African woman.

I admire these books more than I can say. I'd copy them if I could, but I *can't*. I can't even come close. McCall Smith worked for a long time as a Professor of Legal Ethics. He was born in Rhodesia. His soul has qualities and depths I do not have.

Fact or Fiction

Whether you can have *any* fictional material in a memoir is a point that's argued only by people who don't know what they're talking about.

I'd like to make five points about this topic:

1. In writing a memoir you have to cut out nearly all of the true facts about your life. You have to pick and choose a relatively small number of the true parts to include so you can keep your book to a reasonable length. This means that you omit huge swaths of information like your visits to the restroom, details about every meal you've ever eaten in your life.... You get the picture. So, right from the get-go, the book is not a totally accurate depiction of whatever time frame you're writing about. Is that a lie? Is it false? Yes, but the reader wants you to do that.

2. There are times when, totally out of concern for the reader, you might have to add a small number of additional words into a conversation that weren't actually spoken, so as to clarify something that was obvious to both speakers, but will not be known to the reader.

3. There are times when you must conceal the names and identities of characters or locations. Out of respect for the privacy of the individuals you're writing about, you don't use their real names or other identifying information. This is not just about HIPAA—it's about human decency.

4. You don't lie just to make your book sell better. For example, see the opening paragraphs of James Frey's *A Million Little Pieces*. I read the first page

in the bookstore several different times because it was such a huge hit and I wanted to learn from successful books, but I could never make myself buy it because I knew that he'd made it up. It was too staged.

SIDE NOTE: Memoirists can read each others' books and tell what parts of it never happened and also intuit the stuff that's being left out. A knowing reader will learn a lot more about the character of the memoirist than is intentionally presented in the book.

5. You add a very small amount of material that is needed in order for the reader to experience events in the book the same way the character is experiencing them.

Culturally Obscure Material

The Need for "Additional" Material

#5 in the previous section was really hard for me to understand and one of the biggest things I had to grasp. A friend who was an English major and a genius had to teach me about this concept.

Sometimes you can be dealing with a culture or a setting that is virtually unknown to the reader. So you have to take measures to set the scene for them in ways that you would not have to take for a local reader or a reader who is familiar with an unusually private setting. Examples of this are deepest, darkest Appalachia as represented by someone who actually knows what they are talking about, or scenes set in an operating room, or funeral home, by people who actually do that work—not television shows which invariably focus on the shock value of the scene—while professionals are doing the opposite. [This is probably my #1 pet peeve about medical writing. If you are being entertained by the lurid aspects of what is going on, you should be made to leave the room, in my opinion.]

My genius friend read an early draft of *Heart in the Right Place*. He came to me with a serious face, and said, "You can't simply render a literal description of an unusual event and expect a total stranger whose background and life experiences are likely to have been very different from yours and expect them to interpret the situation in the same way that you did."

I had no idea what he was talking about.

"You have to add some *additional material*," he said, "that will set the scene properly for a reader who hasn't had the kind of life you've had and give them a chance to understand *why* you're feeling what you're feeling, doing what you're doing, and why you're having the internal thoughts you're having."

I still had no concept. This is why everyone should write a memoir and give it to a kind friend who happens to be a clinical psychologist.

"You have some really strange situations in here," he said, "so you have to take measures that will allow the reader to experience the action in the same way you did. Or else...."

"Or else what?"

"Or else it's eerie."

"Are you trying to make me feel bad about myself?" I said.

"No. I'm trying to help you not have readers think bad thoughts about you that are inaccurate." He pointed to a particular story and said, "Unless you want them to think you actually have a flat affect, which is not a good thing by the way, you're going to have to build some *on and off-ramps* for people so they will be able to cope with some of these stories."

I handed him a red pen—I used to carry these with me in the old days, because I thought writers were supposed to edit their work with red pens, now I know that any color will do and I've discovered that blue is much less accusatory and a lot more calming. I asked him to put a big red **X** next to the places where I needed an on or off ramp and he was kind enough to do that for me. It was a life-altering lesson.

An example of the sort of thing he was trying to teach me is this: In my world a lot of things that were upsetting or shocking happened all the time. I faced extremely stressful situations that I was powerless to do anything about, coming out of nowhere, on a regular basis from my earliest childhood.

Bloody people frequently popped up in our driveway. Or hysterical parents would run up to me when I was playing in the yard and do things like ask me where my Daddy was while displaying their kid's finger that had been amputated in an accident.

And likewise, things that are totally normal in other families never happened in mine.

The upshot is that I was raised to present an iron-clad poker face and speak in a calm and quiet voice all the time no matter what was going on. I'm a naturally high-strung and hysteria-prone person. On the inside. But on the outside I've had to fake it, for as long as I can remember.

SIDE NOTE: This is why almost nothing on the doctor shows is anything like what happens in real life. TV doctors and nurses are always screaming and shouting. That's not good for a patient. In fact it's counterproductive. But if I wrote the scene flat like it really happened—with the little blond girl exhibiting no apparent hysteria, and no explanation of why that was the case—people would think I was a cold, calculating monster, not just a kid who grew up learning to never raise her voice or act like anything was wrong that Daddy couldn't fix with an aspirin.

I've noticed the same odd emotional control in kids whose parents ran a funeral home. They're able to present a very sober, patient, empathetic facade from childhood.

So, in a memoir, you will occasionally have to inject a few words here and there, not often, maybe a handful of times in the whole book, to help a total stranger who has nothing in common with you experience the events the same way you did.

Confidentiality

In all my books, both fiction and nonfiction, virtually all the characters are real people.

Sometimes friends who appear in my books ask me to obfuscate their identity. I always do my best to do this and sometimes there's a lot of back and forth with the draft manuscript to make sure they feel protected.

And a lot of my books concern incidents that occur in a medical setting, so preserving confidentiality in these situations is paramount.

HIPAA

I never use the names of the real people in the main text of the books in a medical setting (patients or medical personnel or anyone else).

There are a few different techniques that writers use to protect the privacy of people they are writing about. Obfuscation of precise time, location, and physical description can be done as needed.

When this has been done in a nonfiction book you will usually see a notice near the copyright, in the front of the book before the main text begins, that explains what has been done to alter certain details, and why it was done.

I change small details if I think there's *any* chance of identifying a person. If you go read (free with the "Look Inside" feature of Amazon) the disclaimers on the copyright page of the current popular medical memoirs you'll probably see stated there what measures were taken to conceal identities.

It's easier to use the real names and places right up to the last few drafts so you won't confuse yourself about who's who while you're working. But then you can change every name and key identifier on the drafts when you're nearing completion.

The Best Way to
Stay Out of Trouble

The best way to avoid trouble with your memoir is to never say anything mean about another person in print and never make fun of someone in a way you wouldn't want to have done to yourself.

Composite Characters

Another technique to protect the privacy of people you're writing about and who you're putting in vulnerable positions is to use *composite characters*.

Compositing characters can be done to protect people's identities and it can be used to enable you to use small bits of superb material that are too short to stand on their own (and also not complete enough in themselves to be used as one-liners).

I do this occasionally when more than one ranger, doctor, or nurse happens to talk about the same thing, but gives terrific details that the others didn't mention. I do it to flesh out an iconic situation for the benefit of the reader.

My test for myself on matters like this is: Does it honor the reader? Does it provide the reader with a more well-rounded, more mature, understanding of the situation?

Time Compression

In a memoir time can be—and almost always is—tweaked in a couple of different ways.

The time something happened might be intentionally *changed* to conceal some identifying detail. Protecting identities has been extremely important in the medical-related books I've done. I protect the patient, the health care workers, and the facilities involved. It's the way I personally want to do things.

Or, as is especially common in memoirs where you're dealing with an enormous amount of detail spread across a long sweep of time, time might be *compressed*.

This means you cut out the vast number of boring bits of daily life ("I woke up five times during and the night and went to the bathroom twice and almost got up at 5:00 a.m., but went back to sleep…") and focus on the interesting parts without necessarily indicating precisely how much time has passed between one story and the next.

Until you've worked on a memoir you probably haven't thought about how the compression is always there. It's absolutely essential or dealing with the first few minutes of your day could result in a hundred page book.

Ways of dealing with time are done for the purpose of making the narrative less boring, and keep it from running off onto unrelated tangents, while at the same time protecting the identities of the characters.

Things NOT to Do in a Memoir

Cheap Shots, Ridicule, and Snark, Pen Names

Again, this is just me talking. This is what I do, or don't do. In the story of your own life you should always feel free to do as you think best.

Don't *ever* take a cheap shot at anyone in your writing. Just don't do it. EVER.

It's not fair and it won't necessarily come across the way you think it will. No matter how much you'd like to ridicule someone—don't. It may end up making you look like a jerk (or worse).

I love *Vanity Fair*. I absolutely adore the writing style, but in my own work I try to leave out all the snark that you find in their stories. Snark, of course, is what they're famous for and why reading it is such a guilty pleasure. But in a memoir you're writing about your family, friends, people close to you—the VF writers are not.

I also try to leave out all the snide sort of stuff that's embedded a little deeper in the supposedly high-brow publications like *The New Yorker* or essays read on *NPR*. I also try to keep all the embedded political stuff out of my work. To me, it's a potential source of trouble I don't need. Why take a chance irritating readers with irrelevant aspects of your personal subjective thoughts or talking down to them unless that's your reason for writing the piece in the first place?

Vanity Fair, The New Yorker, and *NPR* are beloved for smart writing, but they both carry a tone that reeks of subjective judgments that are being made about the characters without the narrator acknowledging that these comments are simply the opinion of someone who may or may not have been present at the events being described and who may know very little about what they're talking about. A friend of mine calls these *Olympian Pronouncements.*

It's a subtle, or not so subtle culture war, being waged by witty taste-makers and God help you if you belong to a group that isn't currently in style (women, Appalachians, Republicans, gun owners, …).

I might agree with the content of the remark or be amused by it, but I try to be conscious enough of my thoughts that I don't slam people for being overweight or poor, etc. Some of that has undoubtedly seeped out in areas I'm personally blind to, but if so I'm sorry for it.

I despise snarky, bitchy remarks coming from someone who is unaware that they are displaying an ignorant lack of empathy—but love a clever witticism more than anything. It's a fine line and you gotta know your audience.

Oh Gosh I Didn't Realize That Was Perverted!

One of the funniest things you can discover (to your shock and horror) when early drafts of your book are being edited, are blithe statements you make that unwittingly contain goofy, just plain wrong, or even demented or perverted thought patterns or behaviors in yourself, your friends, or your family.

There will come a point when you get an editorial remark and have an uncomfortable double take like, "What? Everyone doesn't do it this way?" Followed instantly by shame, humiliation, and red face.

In my case it kept happening around the fact that I was never asked to give up my career, my life, and stay in Tennessee so I could work as a receptionist and live in my parent's basement in mid-life. Also, I was never thanked for doing it. This disturbed people and their shock baffled me.

Editors kept asking me to put those dramatic and heartwarming family scenes in—the humble request, the gushing gratitude. But because it never happened, I couldn't put it in. That freaked people out. This is when I realized for the first time that other families talked about stuff like that. They had discussions. We didn't. We were *weird*. Even *bizarre*. Oops.

Another example of this happened to a very nice, totally kind, and decent friend who was writing a memoir on child rearing. She found out something she did was considered child abuse by her editor. She would never tell me what it was, but it mortified her that some basic child rearing advice in her book was deemed so perverted by her editor that it had to be stricken. Who knows if anything was actually wrong with the advice? Editing is subjective.

So, realize that your memoir is revealing more to your readers than you can ever know. Until it's published. But then, in addition to all the valid commentary from readers on your many obvious shortcomings you also start getting 13-page handwritten letters on yellow legal-size note paper describing how you stupidly, savagely, and cruelly missed the diagnosis on a patient who would be better off dead than going to your father as their doctor. So get ready.

Or use a pen name.

Pen Names

Using a pen name for a memoir injects a bit of fiction in your nonfiction book.

I fully intended to use a pen name on *Heart in the Right Place* during the entire decade and a half I spent writing it. I had that fantasy right up until the last minute when the publisher insisted that I had to use my real name.

I nearly fainted when that happened.

I had to take a Xanax and go to bed (I take less than one Xanax per year). I have a 25 year old bottle I save for times like this.

The entire time I was writing I had assumed there would be total confidentiality for me, my family, the patients, Strawberry Plains … everything.

But *noooooooooo.*

How to Finish a Project

Keep working on it.
Day in and day out.
Day after day.
For what seems like a long time.
That's the only way to get it done.
Nothing fancy.
Just work.

Fear of Exposing Yourself

Question: Is it difficult to maintain a certain attitude throughout an entire book or is that even necessary? Can you be playful in one chapter and somber in the next? Should you maintain a neutral voice? Is that possible or desired?

Answer: You shouldn't strive to be *neutral*, but you want to be *consistent*. You don't want your text to read like you have multiple personality disorder. This was one of my biggest issues to overcome. Over time you learn to stabilize your narrator/writer voice so you seem knowable and mentally, emotionally, and psychologically stable to the reader. [Unless you're writing as an *unreliable narrator*.]

The gap between *you* and the person depicted in your book is something that has to be explained to everyone who's writing their first memoir. The gap between you and the narrator in your book leads to a funny situation when a reader meets an author face to face. The reader's picture never matches the reality. Humans have moods that vary. A memoir is a tiny slice of a human life. The reader knows about the parts of you that are in the memoir, but that's not *you* as an actual human being.

You want to try to depict your actual personality. You *don't* want to strive to be flat or write with an imaginary fake neutral persona.

But also you'll freeze up if you think writing nonfiction means you have to spill your guts in your memoir. You don't *ever* have to talk about anything you don't want to talk about. You are *always* in total control of what you talk about and what you leave out.

You don't expose yourself in any way that would damage you emotionally. But even when you're trying to be clear and everything you're saying is true, it's still not *you*. It's just a text description of certain parts of you. The person is the book is you as you appear in a text medium talking about specific times and situations.

It's been surreal (startling and/or upsetting) to experience this for myself and then go through the same process with close friends I write with. So far they've all been pleased with the final result. But the process is always nerve-wracking in the early stages of writing and in the first public appearances when you face all the quizzical gazes of "is that *her*"?

Writing a Spiritual Transformation and Recovery Memoir— Advice from MaryAnn Fry

My book was well received because readers felt the experiences that I wrote about, especially the vulnerability. It's as if my words accessed a part of themselves that they couldn't express, but knew. Writing with an authentic voice is critical. Early on, my manuscript was reviewed by D. Patrick Miller of Fearless Literary, and he told me that my writing was powerful, and told me how to tighten it up. Anytime someone teaches you to tighten up your writing, listen. A good book is evocative, and less is more when it comes to ideas in a sentence. Pick an experience, and write about it thoroughly; the room, the people, whatever. Include your inner processes and weave that into the writing seamlessly. Take the reader into the experience.

In order to write from this place within my being, I needed to retreat from the world for a time, and retreat from the good and bad opinions of others. Capture the material first, before you ask for advice. This is what I describe as writing from the belly; following the movement of something alive and real; the creative force. If you do this, readers will feel it, and engage. You are writing into something; not just about something.

Our lives do not resemble the narrative arc of a great fiction book, but you have to have a narrative arc. Organizing the story was much easier when I ended each chapter with a transition sentence at the end. Begin the next chapter with a reference to the subject of the transition. The disjointed parts of a life can come together in a story this way, because truthfully, it's a mystery why I organized the material in the book the way I did. I thank the Muse. There's much more left out of a great book, than included. And, write with active voice; every word counts.

Writing and publishing my Memoir was the most beautiful, alive and courageous endeavor, I've experienced. I wouldn't trade the experience for anything. You must have courage to put forth your work.

MaryAnn Fry is the author of the inspiring memoir *Going Naked, Being Seen: The Power of Being Real,* from Fearless Literary Services, http://www.fearlessbooks.com/Literary.html
https://www.amazon.com/dp/1481215124/

EDITING

What if You Can't Write as Well as __(fill in the blank)__?

The fact that I'll never be able to write as well as my idols doesn't mean I don't have anything of value to contribute.

So don't let your worries about your level of ability stop you from writing.

Highest and Best Use
of the Material

The question you should ask yourself when you're trying to decide what genre, voice, and structure you should write toward is this: What is the highest and best use of this material?

And it's the question you should ask yourself when you're trying to formulate helpful editorial commentary on other people's work as well.

Voice (Again)

There's a complicated mental process involved in turning internal thoughts or spoken language into words that are written to be read. It takes practice. The process feels terribly awkward at first, you're brittle with self-consciousness, but then gradually, with practice, you learn to write prose that sounds like you.

Here's an online dialog I had with a friend about this:

Lisa: I compare what I write to the prose of writers I appreciate. Then I start to write and I wonder how much is really me and how much of my writing is me emulating others—which results in me putting down my pencil.

Carolyn: That's not unusual at first. Every book you read can throw you off in a different direction, very few people have the talent to maintain that imitative trajectory long enough to finish a book with it. If you do, good on ya. But, if you can't maintain the other voice long enough to finish, keep working, and you will overcome the problem.

This is a common issue for beginning writers—that they need to stop reading this or that much admired writer to prevent being drawn off of developing their own voice. You *have* to learn to write in your own voice and stabilize it. Don't worry about having your own quirky style. Readers love a new and distinctive voice.

It took me quite a while to stabilize *me* as read in text. You have to listen to yourself inside your head and see what that sounds like. You're stabilizing a *version* of you, not the *actual* you. Just as a memoir is not really *you*—it's a version of you that you're able to render consistently in print.

In the same way a painting isn't exactly what the person looks like—it's what a subjective static image of them looks like when it's painted by a particular artist. Your writing voice will always show technique or brush strokes that are specific to you. But it's always an artificial thing you develop over time and learn to stabilize. It's hard work.

When I was first starting (and for years afterwards) I would try to write like Gregory McDonald, or Leslie Thomas, or James Herriot, or Alexander McCall Smith, for example, until I finally realized I was never going to be able to succeed. I'm no Gregory McDonald, Leslie Thomas, James Herriot, or Alexander McCall Smith. I was forced to write in my own voice for lack of any other choice.

But at first you don't know what your own voice sounds like on paper. You have to work that out with yourself.

It's a gradual process.

Lisa: If I'm not passionate about what I am writing I think it will be without value. I have an unrealistic concept of what writing a memoir is.

I can teach my students how to write creatively and to be patient knowing their writing will improve with practice. I just have to believe it for myself.

Carolyn: The totally unglamorous and honest truth is that I never aspired to be a writer. Even now I don't think of myself as a writer. I just happen to write for a living. I had to learn how to write when I had no other options to feed myself. To me it's not fun. It's just work like digging a ditch. One shovelful at a time. There's no glamour or thrill to it for me. Just work.

Lisa: My unrealistic concept is that if I am not swept away with my writing it must be pretty bad. Picture one of the scenes from *Amadeus* when Mozart is working on a new opera. Or Joan from *Romancing the Stone* when she is exhausted and emotional upon completion of her novel. I will get beyond my fanciful ideas. I will start again one shovelful at a time.

Roller Coaster Moments

Here's a conversation about dealing with the highs and lows of writing a long form narrative.

Betty: When you wrote your first book, did you have roller coaster moments? I mean for a while did you think, *Man this is gonna be great! I can't wait till it's done!* to rereading what you wrote and thinking, *Who would want to take the time to read this?* If so how did you handle the highs and lows?

Carolyn: Great question. Yes, I had highs and lows—a lot of them. You have allow yourself to get high, to like your work in progress or you'll never finish it. And when you're finished, or periodically during the writing process, you'll inevitably notice that your work could benefit from editing and you'll need to keep going back to rework it to make it best you can.

Any and all artistic effort is a roller coaster experience. This is especially true and something you have to learn to deal with on a prolonged project like writing a book.

My personal secret to mood management is cookies and a *lot* of Diet Coke. Lots of sugar and tons of caffeine are the only way I can get any writing done whatsoever.

The good news is that when you're done with your manuscript a lot of extremely fun things will crop up like when you hear a good narrator perform the text you wrote and add their own talent to the words. In times like that you can find yourself thinking you're a pretty good writer. LOL.

Also it's important to understand that for every book on earth—some people will love it and some people will hate it. There's no book in the world that *every* person will enjoy or *every* person will think is awful.

Always remember that you're writing for the people who will like to know about whatever it is that you're writing about (your dog Ollie in your case). And that's good enough. Plenty of people will enjoy knowing about Ollie. But at the same time some people could never like a book about a wonderful dog, no matter who wrote it. You're not writing for those people. This is just reality. And it's okay.

Space to Exist

The protagonist of one of my all-time favorite books, *A Gentleman in Moscow* by Amor Towles, provides what I think is a perfect representation of what memoirists are searching for in their own work.

Although *A Gentleman in Moscow* is a work of fiction, it's all about developing an inner life—a physical, intellectual, emotional, and psychological space to exist in, as yourself—so you can tolerate the external conditions you're forced to live in.

We write memoir to build ourselves a calm, safe, organized space to *be*, so we can survive, and indeed thrive, in whatever our circumstances are.

Memoir is a deep spiritual process. It's one of the most worthwhile adventures you can ever undertake.

Bad Reviews, Unhelpful Feedback, Advice You Can't Take

How do you handle criticism, rejection, editing?

Nobody enjoys being criticized (or maybe I'm naïve and there are people out there who do), but if you're one of the ones who don't enjoy being critiqued by well-meaning people (and clueless people and mean-spirited people) you have to learn to handle negative comments about your work like a pro if you're gonna work on a book and stay in the game long enough to finish it.

Especially if you're dealing with a traditional publisher. And again after your book is published.

Bad Reviews

At first, bad reviews are like a stake through your heart. Some writers never get over being massively traumatized by them. If you're successful you'll get hundreds, then thousands, of reviews. For your own safety you need to learn how to cope with the commentary of strangers about the people and places and thoughts that are the most dear to your heart.

The honest truth is that *a review says a lot more about the reviewer than it does the writer.*

You have to embed this concept in the forefront of your brain and use it to protect your heart. Wear it as your shield. Don't ever take it off.

IMPORTANT ADVISORY: Never never never, I mean *never*, respond to a bad review. Leave it laying there, smoking, steaming .... and move on with your life. Responding in any way whatsoever to a bad review will just makes things worse. The reviewer wanted to hurt you and if you respond they'll know they succeeded. They'll enjoy knowing they succeeded and are typically spring-loaded to go for Round 2 if you give them the slightest opportunity.

Every writer I know, including me, had to learn this the hard way. There will be a review that we just *can't* leave alone. In my case it was an attack on my elderly parents that in hindsight I shoulda ignored. But instead I toiled over my response for way too long, posted it, and then BAM. Okay, now I get it. NEVER respond to a bad review.

Even if you enjoy arguing and wrangling as your favorite sport, any back and forth between you and your reviewer will reveal nothing edifying about either participant to the spectators (who are your potential customers).

Some writers claim to never read any of their reviews. I seriously doubt this is true for anyone. But if it is, I sincerely hope that approach works for them.

I try to read each and every one of my reviews. Even the mean ones. I wanna learn whatever I can from reviews. It's the only contact I'll ever be able to have with most of my readers, so I treasure the opportunity to get the feedback. The bad reviews still sting and sometimes I can't help making frustrated snappy comebacks in my mind, but I keep those to myself and often try to send up a quick non-sarcastic prayer for the misguided curmudgeon who had the gall to criticize my writing.

If none of this advice is working for you so far—the funniest thing to do immediately after getting a terrible review is to think of your most beloved handful of books, books that you treasure, and go read some of the 1-star reviews on those books. It will put things into perspective. It never fails to make me smile no matter how upset I was when I started.

You can also click on the profile for the person who gave you a bad review and discover that this person gives bad reviews on nearly every book they read. Or if not every book, then notice the ones they give 5-stars. I guarantee those will make you roll your eyes. This will demonstrate that you have differing tastes. Again, this will give you a healthy context for bad reviews.

Reviews are *subjective* even when they come from an expert (or a *so-called* expert). Even nice, kind people who are trying to help you will give you dumb, painful, useless feedback.

Reviews will often contain a projection from inside the reviewer that has nothing whatsoever to do with what you wrote, but if you take the time to mull over the comment anyway you might wonder if there are a lot of other people out there who have the same outlook on life as the person who made the idiotic comment, and you might go back and add a word to two to your manuscript to fend off this particular misconception.

Or not.

If the fix is easy and doesn't ruin the story, maybe you wanna do it. Comedy is particularly delicate with pacing and rhythm, so some fixes might ruin the joke, but maybe you can adjust something minor and still preserve the entertainment value of your prose.

You can get tricked into responding to a review. The review might say something like: "If there's one thing I hate it's a book where the purple pony gets tortured. This book went there and the description was so graphic, so disgusting, the writer should be committed to a mental institution. Don't read this book unless you want to vomit."

If you innocently reply to the review and say, "Forgive me, but there is no purple pony, no ponies of any color, or torture of any kind in my book. My book is a primer on quilt making." They will attack you again. It's virtually guaranteed.

I have trouble getting Amazon to remove book reviews like this: "I hate this potato peeler with a passion. It broke the first time I tried to use it!!!! 1-star."

Unhelpful Feedback

You want to be careful letting family, loved ones, or any unqualified person read your early drafts. Amateur reviewers will often be full of advice, all of it useless. *Never* give your book to an amateur who doesn't like the genre you're writing in. And don't give it to people who don't read in the genre you're aiming for.

If you do you'll be getting nothing but inappropriate stylistic suggestions, useless projections, or attempted makeovers into a genre you're not writing in. For me, the last straw that enabled me to learn this lesson forever was when a close friend said, and this was *all* he said: "Well, … it isn't Tolstoy."

That comment felt like a nail gun to the head. This was said at an important stage of working on *Heart in the Right Place* when I'd first gotten a coherent draft of the whole thing. I was jobless, hopeless, desperate, and not trying to write like Tolstoy anyway. I don't even *like* Tolstoy. I know lots of people do. I've read some of it. I don't hate it, but it's not anything I would ever aim for with my own writing. Even twenty years later I'm still freaked out about this type of unhelpful dirty-bomb commentary. Do you say to your child when they show you their little handprint in red paint, "Well, … it isn't Michelangelo."

You gotta get a thick skin or you'll never make it to the finish line.

So, in summary, during the early stages of working on your memoir, unless the comments are coming from a pro who is working in same the genre you're in, or from a voracious reader in that genre, go with your own judgement.

Advice You Can't Take

Always be prepared to disregard feedback from anyone and everyone. If the advice helps, use it. If not, fuggedaboudit.

I've saved this type of comment for last because it's the type of critique that makes me particularly sad—not angry, just depressed: A person you respect (or it's even worse when it's a person you can't stand) gives you great advice that you cannot take because you're *unable* to take it.

"You need to make this book less/more ____" (fill in the blank with anything you're utterly incapable of doing).

The person is pointing out something that's true and wise and with all your heart you want to take the advice, but you *can't* because you don't have the *ability,* the talent, to take it. Your writing skills aren't sufficient to the task.

The advice is, in essence, to correct the weakest point in your writing. You know the comment is spot on. You wish, you pray, that you could remedy the defect, but it's never gonna happen. Or at least not soon.

My Favorite 1-Star Reviews

I've learned to enjoy all my reviews—good, bad, and indifferent. At least they indicate someone read my book and bothered to say something about it.

My current favorite bad book review said something along the lines of this (I tried to find the exact wording, but discovered you can't word-search reviews):

"This is nothing but a bunch of stories from radiologists about doing their jobs!!" — said about my book entitled *Radiologists at Work: Saving Lives with the Lights Off.*

Here's another of my favorite bad reviews:

"She thanked like 15 or 20 people at the end of the book. Who does that?!"

My Editing Kit

Caffeine — largest possible container of Diet Coke — Krystal Roadie with *light ice* is the largest I can find. McDonalds is my favorite though.

Writing an Animal Rescue Activist Memoir—Advice from C.A. Wulff

When I wrote my first book, *Born Without a Tail*, a memoir told in short stories, I didn't know anything about writing professionally. I just knew that there were stories that I wanted to remember about my family of pets. I learned a lot along the way that I am happy to share with you here. Whether you are writing a memoir or fiction, I hope you'll find my tips helpful.

1. Write the way you speak. It will keep your narrative flowing naturally and your voice will be more authentic. You can go back later and correct any grammatical errors.

2. Don't let adjectives or too much description get in the way of your message. Flowery language gunks up the works. You can add descriptors in subsequent drafts if something is too stark or sparse.

3. Avoid "filler" and vague words like: really, about, never/always, almost/nearly, all/every, additionally, believe/feel, currently, finally, often/frequently, and very.

4. A rough outline or a simple list of subjects you want to touch on, will help keep you organized and focused.

5. If you already have a title, refer back to it as a guide to help you stay on point.

6. It's perfectly OK to change people's names in your story. You may want to do that to avoid making someone angry or to protect someone's privacy or reputation. I used fictitious names for the

veterinarians in both of my pet memoirs, because when I wrote about vet visits and diagnosis, I was quoting from memory. I didn't want to attribute any mis-remembered information to a real vet. Likewise, when I wrote about family members who I felt were poor pet owners, I turned them into fictitious friends in my books.

7. Be flexible with your time line if it helps to organize your story.

8. A good story will make the reader feel something. Nobody wants to feel sad 100% of the time, so think about your target audience: Ask yourself "why would someone want to read this?" That should help you refrain from being overly maudlin. People love to laugh. Can you find something funny about the story you are writing?

9. Spell Check, but don't stop there (their or they're!) Proofread. Proofread again. Have someone else proofread. Read your text aloud to your dog. Reading aloud catches errors you may miss during initial proofreading.

10. Grow a thick skin, you'll need it for rejection letters and the inevitable bad reviews. No matter how brilliant you, your story, or your writing is, there will still be people who don't like it. Don't take their criticism personally.

C. A. Wulff, is the author of *Born Without a Tail, How to Change the World in 30 Seconds, Circling the Waggins, Parade of Misfits,* and *Finding Fido.*

In addition to being a writer, she is an artist and animal advocate.

Come join her Up on The Woof!
thewoof.wordpress.com or visit her author page on Amazon at
https://www.amazon.com/default/e/B002BRH03K/

PUBLISHING

Indie vs Traditional Publishing

When you're trying to decide whether to try to get traditionally published or publish your work independently it's important to listen to people who are so-called *hybrid* authors—writers who have been both traditionally published and independently published.

Both traditional publishing and indie publishing are undergoing constant and rapid change. The world of publishing is morphing daily. For several years now it has been evolving to reduce the appeal of traditional publishing and increase the appeal of independent publishing.

There *used* to be a stigma against indie-publishing/self-publishing/vanity-publishing (call it what you want) until this year when the sales of indie-pubbed books overtook the sales of all of the traditional publishers put together.

For several years indie books have often earned spots atop national sales charts. And indie books are also often as highly-rated, if not higher-rated, by readers than traditionally published books.

I've been contacted a bunch of times by Hollywood on several of my indie published books.

Indie publishing is crushing the traditional publishing industry. Literary agents are going out of business. Publishing houses are going out of business. Chain bookstores are going out of business.

Indie book sales are skyrocketing in all formats.

The biggest attractions of traditional publishing are:

Perceived status, assistance of professionals in producing a final product, and savvy marketing assistance.

There is *some* truth to these perceptions, but the truth doesn't come anywhere near matching the perception unless you're one of the handful of very top-tier writers like Grisham, Baldacci, King, etc. And despite the fact that they're able to intervene in the publishing of their own books in a way a typical author is not allowed to, plenty of top authors have been known to change publishers, too. There will be a good reason they did it.

The biggest drawbacks to traditional publishing are:

If you're writing a memoir and you go to a traditional publishing house you will lose control of your own life story *for the rest of your life.*

You will be paid less than a fifth of what you'd be paid by if you self-publish and you will be paid *many* months after the money is earned. The royalty percentages vary from hardback, to softcover, to ebook, to audio, but you lose a great deal of income from your work by being traditionally published.

You will have no control over the pricing or marketing of your book. People who don't know you and don't particularly care about you will *restrict* you from interfering in what is typically *2 weeks of marketing.*

It will take at least a year, if not two, from the time your book is sold to the publisher before it is actually published.

Agents and traditional publishers require you produce some extremely arduous documentation (a 75-page book proposal, for example) that takes time away from your efforts to write an actual book.

You will have soul-destroying experiences. Don't make me tell you what they are.

Please stop and think about this before worrying about getting an agent and selling your book to a traditional publisher.

If you succeed in getting an agent and a traditional publisher your experience will not be what you're picturing. Instead you're likely to be headed for some of the rudest shocks of your life. You're likely to be throwing yourself and your book away on a dream that isn't real.

It's bad enough if we're talking about all this in the context of a work of fiction, but when it's happening to you around a memoir …. (shudder).

Writers who are making huge money in indie publishing have horror stories. Sadistic stories. That's why they changed to indie publishing. Not because they couldn't get agents and publishers, but because they *did* and saw what happened!

Several people I know, and I, have made six-figure income on a book or books that traditional publishers rejected as *not of publishable quality* or *no good*. Several nice people I know are making seven-figure incomes on rejected or improperly marketed books that they had to buy back their rights to, or sue to get the rights reverted, so they could sell it themselves.

I've heard many things that defy belief and yet I know they're true. These things really happened to innocent writers. Some of the things happened to me. Bad things. Heartbreaking things.

Writers used to not be able to speak about these things, even to each other, because the traditional houses had a monopoly and they were known to be retaliatory and vindictive. But now the monopoly is crumbling, the gag is off, and indie writers are telling each other *everything* and *helping* each other. It's an amazing community.

Nowadays, many of the same professionals who would work on various aspects of your book at a traditional house—like editing, layout, cover design, and marketing—are available for hire. And you can keep up to 70% of your royalties instead of 12% or so from a traditional publisher, with similar ratios for print books. And instead of no audio book at all or a flat fee for the audio book, you can have terrific professional narrators do them via Amazon ACX and make 25%-40% on each copy sold.

If you still want to go with a traditional publishing house … you must do as you think best.

But ask yourself if you're willing to hand off your book, your life story, *forever*

1. for validation from people who will not treat you the way you are imagining
2. or because you don't want to have to handle details like hiring excellent, affordable, and readily available formatting or cover assistance, or do your own marketing
3. because you have a fantasy about being pampered like a prima donna artiste and having other people do all these things for you [Insider Tip: *that's not gonna happen.*]

Agents

How do you find an agent?

You want to be careful about how you initiate contact with a potential agent. Agents generally maintain the stance of an irritable guard who's constantly repelling invaders.

This is because strangers are bombarding them all the time with projects that are not likely to be anything they want to represent. Agents are trying to sip from a firehose.

Because of this I picture them hurling insults over the wall like the French soldiers in Monty Python. Watch this two-minute clip to get a sense of the tone of the conversation you'll have with a potential agent: https://www.youtube.com/watch?v=QSo0duY7-9s

Agents, although they're not optimistic, they need to find the occasional project to represent if they're going to make a living, so if you show professionalism in how you approach them, that will help you break through the noise.

To find an agent, you can write or email them (depending on what *they* prefer, not what *you* prefer), or you might get a referral through a friend who will tell you how to make contact, or you could attend a workshop where agents have agreed to listen to people pitch book projects to them. Don't call an agent unless requested to.

Comical aside: A hugely famous agent called me once and when he said his name I screamed and spastically clenched the phone so hard it flew across the room like a watermelon seed. When the handset hit the floor it hung up on him. I hadn't managed to say any actual words aside from *Hello*. I'd just barked out an incredibly loud inarticulate noise and fumbled the phone airborne.

The famous agent gave me a minute to get hold of myself, called back, and introduced himself again without indicating in any way that the previous idiotic event had occurred. That's class. Obviously I wasn't the first writer who'd had that reaction when being direct-dialed without advance warning.

If you're writing an agent to try to get representation, you'll have to send what's called a *query* that contains a very concise version of your credentials and a very concise pitch for your book. Never send an agent a manuscript or an excerpt from your manuscript unless they ask you to.

If you send them a manuscript they've requested, be sure to write on the outside of the mailing container *REQUESTED MANUSCRIPT*.

There is advice all over the web and in many how-to books about how to write a query letter. It's a letter that will include your elevator pitch, your credentials, your existing media platform, and demonstrate by its very nature how well you write and how good you are at selling your book (to the agent and to the world in general which will become important if and when your book is published).

If you're talking to the agent in person or on the phone you need a really good elevator pitch for your book and it needs to be catchy, distinctive, and original.

Do not scare the agent. Don't stalk. Don't back the agent into a corner in a room or elevator. Don't follow them into a restroom and pitch your book while they are relieving themselves.

Editors

How do you find an editor?

Indie author groups on Yahoo and Facebook will give recommendations for the various types of editors: Acquisition, Developmental, Content, Copy, Line, Proofreader, ...

The type of editor you need depends on how far along you are with your manuscript. Here are a couple of nice summaries of the various types of editors:
http://thehelpfulwriter.com/kinds-of-editors-what-editors-do/index.html
https://www.grammarly.com/blog/amandaonwriting-four-types-of-book-editing-1/

There are lots of freelancers out there who do editing and you can get recommendations from writers in the indie online groups.

I want my books to be professional, but I'm not trying to impress anyone with my literary talent (and some people would say it shows). I grew up as a huge fan of *Readers Digest* and that's the reading level I'm comfortable with. Also I come from a family and a region where budgetary constraints are very tight as a hallmark of our culture. Because I aim for zero overhead in my book publishing I'm reluctant to shell out thousands, or even hundreds, of dollars for editing.

Momma and some really smart and kind Facebook friends have been my indie editors so far. I prefer to keep things informal. Nearly twenty years ago I hired a "book doctor" I found online for broad, general, overall advice and got some good and some not-so-good suggestions. One was, "Kill your mother in the opening scene. That will make you seem like a more sympathetic character for the whole rest of the book."

I reminded the book doctor that this was a memoir, nonfiction, and he said, "Oh, yeah, right."

Nevertheless I gamely (in total desperation and without telling Momma) tried a draft with Momma's funeral as the opening scene. Momma went against my explicit instructions and sneaked a peek at the safety backup copy of the manuscript I kept in her office on CD in a sealed envelope and saw it and got really upset and never read another word of *Heart in the Right Place*.

Many years after the book doctor experience I was asked by an agent to pay $8,000 to have a very nice and talented person take a look at *Heart In the Right Place* and make comments. Then a large number of the suggested edits were rejected by the agent. I still love both of the professional editors who tried to help me, even though it was largely a counterproductive exercise from my point of view and cost me large sums that I had to borrow from my parents.

Nowadays I would love to have a great professional *story* editor, but now I'd feel confident having a back and forth with them about my taste versus their taste. That's what a high level of editing comes down to anyway. And I'd want to be in a position where I could take or leave the advice.

Editing is a very high skill, a very specialized skill, and not many people are great at it. We're not talking about copyediting and correcting punctuation here. It's a wonderful thing to experience it at a high level. My agent had the high level of skill. My editor at Algonquin had the high level of skill. But in the future I want to have more of a say about which bits of advice to take and which to ignore.

I don't ever want to go back to not having the last word about the story of my own life.

Bad editors will simply rewrite your material by imposing their own personal style onto your manuscript. That's annoying because you can't sustain it. It's their voice, not yours. It's not helpful if you hope to have a writing career. You'll eventually need to learn to write in your own style.

Contracting with Independent Professionals

When you finish your manuscript you can work with a wide range of professionals who independently contract with writers. You can get some of the same professionals who work with the traditional publishers if you want.

Editing

You can hire any of a wide range of *types* of editing as described earlier.

Savvy close friends of mine have had great results with the editors at Polgarus Studio in Tasmania https://www.polgarusstudio.com (*I receive no incentive for this recommendation*)

Formatting

Your book manuscript might originate in Microsoft Word, Pages, Scrivener, Vellum, or other format. You'll need to have it converted to other formats for publishing in print or ebook for the various online stores such as Amazon, B+N, Kobo, and iTunes, among others.

You can upload several different formats directly, so this might be a simple process for you, depending on what format your original manuscript is in, what formats you know how to work with, what formats you can convert yourself, what format you want to sell a final product in, and what stores you want to upload to.

But even if you can master the reformatting yourself, it's not always easy to upload your final covers and text to some of the online vendors. iTunes is notorious for a quirky, nonsensical interface and terrible (no) customer service. Amazon's ebook interface (KDP) is easy and has wonderful customer service. Nook and Kobo are in the middle. But for iTunes I had to cave and get help. Now I have an expert and economical professional service do the formatting and uploading (except to Amazon, which I can do myself).

I am massively relieved since I started working with Jason Anderson of Polgarus Studio in Tasmania https://www.polgarusstudio.com for all my formatting and difficult uploading. I used to do it myself, but it's really stressful for me and I'm not the greatest at it. So finally I decided to try Jason and it's was a Godsend for me, especially as I got more and more books published. *(Not getting a discount for recommending Jason — this is totally sincere)*

There are also free or economical tools you can get to help with conversion and uploading like Calibre, Vellum, Scrivener, among others. Technically iBooks falls into this category, but if you can figure out how to use that interface I will bow down to your mastery of technology.

Formatting can also include the interior book design. An ebook is a special critter where lines have to *flow* because the reader might be using different font sizes or different screen orientations. There are different design parameters for how the inside looks. Different brands of ereaders have certain default fonts, for example. So there are things to know about how to create an ebook, especially the Table of Contents with the jump links to the beginnings of the chapters. You might not need jump links if you're writing fiction, but they are customary for nonfiction.

The design of the interior of the book—fonts, layout, headers and footers, page numbering, for example—is an art. It is especially important for the PDF that will be uploaded for your print version. Some programs like Vellum help you create a nice looking book from your Word document. But if you're using a formatting service they can address this issue for you.

I'm fortunate to be friends with an excellent book designer, so I can get first-rate advice about the look of the inside of the printed book. What I've learned is that some people like cream colored pages, some prefer white. Some people like glossy book covers, some prefer matte finish.

Opinions on font styles and font sizes vary. I like 14 point serif fonts because I'm old (and I'm not the only one because 14 point is the Kindle default font size). I've heard that 80% of book buyers are middle-aged and older women.

But to young people 14 point fonts look like a book for the visually impaired.

Cover Design

Cover design for ebooks is much simpler than for print. Print covers can be made in a wide range of sizes and aspect ratios. But they all require a higher resolution (300 dpi) image than the ebook (72 dpi), as well as a front cover, back cover, and spine that fits the templates of the various print-on-demand (POD) companies and online stores.

I can create a final ebook cover myself (if I need to) using the monthly PhotoShop license and a MacBookPro. But creating these covers at a professional looking level (which is imperative if you want your book to sell) often requires skill with Adobe InDesign, Illustrator, PhotoShop, or some other sophisticated software.

I did my own ebook cover designs initially, then as I got more confidence in indie publishing I began to send them to a graphic design expert for comments, suggestions, adjustments, and production of the design concept into the different sizes and formats I need.

But even now I always work hard to do the original design myself and get a lot of feedback from Facebook friends on various draft cover concepts rather than going to an artist with a blank slate, because it speeds up the process. The trial covers can be tested for the content and tone they convey and for any implications that I might not be aware of.

The audio book cover has to be done separately because it has a different aspect ratio from a print or ebook cover. It's square in keeping with CD covers.

Cover Image Rights

There are several reasonably priced stock photo agencies (and some insanely expensive ones). I generally use ShutterStock or iStockPhoto. Or, because I know a lot of fantastic wildlife and landscape photographers, I buy the rights to use an image directly from them (as I have several times from Bill Lea and Donna Eaton, for example).

Audio Books

The best place to create your audio book is ACX.com which is owned by Amazon.

You can post an excerpt of your manuscript and audition narrators through ACX until you find someone you like.

You can pay narrators two ways—either a 50-50 split of royalties or by the finished hour of the recorded book. You can produce the audio yourself or have the narrator do it.

I've always done the 50-50 split because that seems more fair to me, it's low overhead (which is always a big concern) and also I enjoy working with partners.

Writing can be a solitary endeavor. It's pleasant to engage with other people anywhere I can along the way. And getting to hear your book rendered by a great narrator is *fun*!

ACX customer service is not good (my only complaint about them). Fortunately, I've rarely needed any customer service from them.

FYI, high-quality audio recording and editing is extremely time-consuming, so you want to get an expert for this. Don't try to do it yourself or with a rank amateur unless you have the right equipment and skills.

Multiplicity of Formats and Vendors

Over time you can get quite a large number of books to keep track of on account of the multiplicity of formats and vendors.

Print Hardcover – (PDF, Adobe Photoshop, Illustrator, InDesign)
Print Softcover – (PDF, Adobe Photoshop, Illustrator, InDesign)
Audio – (mp3)
Ebook Amazon – (mobi)
Ebook B+N Nook – (epub)
Ebook Kobo – (epub)
Ebook iTunes – (epub)
Original Manuscript – (Word, Pages, Scrivener, Vellum)

So there are likely to be loaded covers and interiors for:
3 text formats (paperback, audio, ebook)
4 vendors (Amazon, B+N, Kobo, iTunes)
= 12 uploads

If you have several books out, it really adds up quickly.

In my case it's 12 x 14 books = 168 books

Writing for Different Arenas— Advice from Jeremy Blachman

I haven't written a memoir, but maybe I have. My first novel, *Anonymous Lawyer*, was inspired by my summer as a law firm associate, while I was a student at Harvard Law School. It began as a blog, where I wrote in the fictional guise of a middle-aged law firm hiring partner. The character was invented and exaggerated, but the emotions were real, and buried in the writing was one character, a young law student trying to figure out if this was the path he wanted to follow — and he was absolutely the stand-in for me and my own experiences, my fears, my reality. When the book was published, I worried that the people I'd met that summer would recognize themselves in print. As far as I'm aware, they didn't — but under oath, I think I'd have to admit there was more truth in the pages than fiction. It wasn't a memoir, but your memoir doesn't have to be either — for me, fiction has allowed me to use my life, but only as much as I want to. The fun part, sometimes, is figuring out what would have made reality even better — even more rewarding for the reader — than it actually was.

Since *Anonymous Lawyer* was published, most of my writing has fallen somewhere in that space between fiction and non-fiction. I adapted Anonymous Lawyer for television with NBC, though it never aired, and there were versions of the script that ended up turning my book on its head, making me the main character instead of the fictional law firm partner I'd invented, seeing the world through my eyes instead of his. I wrote a second novel, *The Curve*, about a corrupt, for-profit law school, with a co-author who had experience as a law school professor. He wrote the professor parts, I wrote the student parts, and we used our experiences to inform the story. Much closer to memoir, last year I wrote a series of posts on Medium about the premature birth of my son — the experience of the neonatal intensive care unit, of his fragility — and of my fragility in trying to cope. The difference between writing those posts as memoir and the work I've done as fiction was far less than I expected it would be. The emotions are real, regardless of the form, and your experiences come out in the writing regardless of whether you decide to stay true to the facts or not.

As a ghostwriter and editor, I've helped a number of clients get their stories onto the page — memoir, corporate history, self-help, life-inspired novels — and the questions are the same, no matter the form. What really made you feel something? What do you have a passion to share? What is most meaningful about your experiences? I've worked with professionals who think it's all about the chronological narrative — what they accomplished, who they met, where they went. But, honestly, it's not. It's about how they felt, what they wished for, what went right and what went wrong. I helped one entrepreneur with a book proposal — his story should have been amazing, the things he'd accomplished in a few short years, the ups and downs of a growing company, the almost-disasters, the inflection point where things started to turn around, the ultimate triumph of success. But he had trouble letting me in — or maybe there just wasn't that much to let me in to see. It was all too easy for him, emotionally. He never doubted, or so he said. He never regretted, or so he said. He never truly felt emotionally invested, or so it seemed. And so on the page, ultimately, I had to amplify his struggle, or at least that's what I felt like I was doing. It was memoir, and the facts were real, but I'm not sure it wasn't leaning ever-so-slightly toward fiction, the more emotional life I gave him, the more internal drama I tried my best to create within the boundaries of the truth.

My current project is a novel about fatherhood that started out as a memoir about fatherhood — and it largely is a memoir about fatherhood, at least so far, but I'm protecting myself by calling it fiction, I think. I'm protecting myself from fully admitting — to myself and to others — that the emotions on the page are real, and not just exaggerated for the reader. That's probably a mistake, but it's better than the alternative — to hold back, to guard, to worry about the consequences of what you're writing. If you're worried about the consequences, call it fiction. You'll still know it's real — and, most important, the reader will get all of the emotions, and not just the ones you feel safe sharing. Good writing isn't safe, or at least I've found that my own writing is best when I worry — whether fiction or not — that perhaps I've said too much. Good luck.

Jeremy Blachman lives in Scarsdale, NY, with his wife and two sons. He is the author of two novels, *Anonymous Lawyer* and *The Curve* (co-authored with Cameron Stracher), both of which have been developed for television with NBC. Read more of his writing at jeremyblachman.com, or contact him at jeremy.blachman@gmail.com.

MARKETING

Indie Marketing

What marketing do you do?

The best available options and methods for marketing indie books are changing all the time. Best practices can change daily, so you have to keep up with what's working this week. This is why indie writers talk amongst themselves a lot.

At the moment the most effective and best return on investment comes from buying ads for your ebook with the discount ebook enewsletters. The bigger the mailing list that the enewsletter has for readers in your genre the better. The Big Kahuna is BookBub. BookBub is an awesome resource. But you can stack a lot of smaller ads on the same day or over several days and that can work reasonably well, too.

The lists of the discount ebook enewsletters changes over time. Indie writers share the morphing lists with friends on social media and Facebook or Yahoo Groups, for example.

There are all sorts of free ebook giveaway strategies, too. Some of them are complex with middlemen like BookFunnel delivering the ebook for you in an automated and (you hope) safer way that prevents further online free dissemination without your permission.

SIDE NOTE: Piracy. All of my books have been massively pirated. I like J.A. Konrath's view (read his blog on publishing, it's wonderful) that the people who download your book from a pirate site would never have paid for it anyway, so be glad to get another customer any way you can. Also, many of the sites that appear to offer pirated ebooks for free are actually phishing sites, so the people stealing, or hoping to steal, your book are instead getting identity theft. That seems fair.

The biggest way to offer your book for free is on BookBub. It takes nerves of steel to give away 50,000 or 100,000 books for free, but it can also successfully launch a book and a career. If a book is not selling well, what difference does it make if you give it away to get it seen and reviewed? This makes even more sense if you have other books out. If the reader liked the free book, maybe they'll go buy some of your other books.

There are many ways to give books away. The methodology changes frequently, so by the time you're ready to try this you'll have to ask some successful indie writers what they are currently recommending.

Social media helps you advertise a book. And an author website helps. An appealing author page on Amazon is *extremely important*. An author page on BookBub is a good idea, too. And an author page on GoodReads.

Some people buy Google ads, Facebook ads, and/or Amazon ads. These ads work reasonably well for some people, but not so much for others. Marketing is an art and science.

Tactics may vary across genres.

If you're writing to make a living the odds favor you if you write a great mystery or romance series and keep producing excellent books in that series.

In theory you want your book to be reviewed in the media. You can go on radio shows, TV shows, make YouTube videos, put out podcasts. It's a lot of work and you have to keep doing it if you want a career. If you pay for professional PR assistance, it's super-expensive. I've never been able to afford it and I'm horribly camera shy anyway [trauma increased a thousandfold by a kid who somehow combined terrible lighting, awful camera angle, lying to me by assuring me that I was only being filmed from the mid-chest upward, and having me sit in a broken chair to produce YouTube video where I look like I weigh 400 pounds instead of 140. It's a worst case scenario for any woman.]

There's no end to marketing gambits. If you can afford to hire someone to do all the marketing, that would be ideal. Very few authors can afford that.

My maximum expenditure so far, for total costs in indie-publishing any of my 12 books, is around $500. For the first one, *Medicine Men* it was $120.

The Importance of a Great Title

The most important things about your book are the title, subtitle, and cover.

The buying decision is often made from the cover. Great covers will sell mediocre or even awful books. Great covers will make millionaires out of people whose writing is *bad*.

The title, subtitle, and cover of your book needs to be as catchy as possible and at the same time convey a general idea of the content of the book as well as the tone.

And in 4th place I'd put the first paragraph or first half page of the book, and in 5th place a snappy review or a lot of high ratings.

Think of how you decide what books to buy. It's highly likely to be from a quick scan of these few items.

Titles and Subtitles

Selecting your title and subtitle may take a lot of work and the search will likely go on until the very last minute. Anyone who knows me knows I go through a long process of thinking up a lot of possible titles and then vetting them with anyone who will give me their opinion.

It's very important to test your titles and see what strangers think the book is about. You don't want to accidentally make your book seem different from what it really is. An accidental (or intentional) bait and switch will generate ruinous reviews.

More modern considerations in titling and subtitling are computer search engines. If possible, you want to include the most popular and accurate key words in your title and subtitle, so the right shoppers can find your book easily, and online stores will get them *shelved* in the right category.

You will be able to indicate a category or several categories to the online stores, but if you can, use the title and subtitle to ensure your book shows up on searches in your subject matter.

Titles are not copyrightable in the U.S. so if you want you can name your book *Star Wars* or *Gone With the Wind*.

SIDE NOTE: There's a bit of a stink going on right now because a porno-ish author is attempting to block all other porno-ish writers (and chicken farmers or writers about insolent people) from using the word "cocky" in their book titles. She's apparently pretty aggressive and litigious (and legally wrong) so a gang of indie authors organized themselves and are contesting this.

The woman will lose her lawsuits because unless you're using the same title for the purpose of confusing people into buying your book when they think they're buying the other person's, it's fine to have similar titles.

It's not okay to have two books with the same title if they have the same or extremely similar subject matter. But you cannot copyright a *word* and say no one else can use that word unless you invented the word yourself. And even then, there are exceptions. You can only trademark a word under certain circumstances and not if it's in common parlance. You can't just stake out the word "the" and sue anyone else who uses it.

Do some title research when you get ideas. Run your proposed titles and subtitles on Amazon and see what pops up. And run them on Google and see what you get. You might find previous titles you don't want to duplicate or associations you don't want to make because they're misleading.

I used to go out of my way to think up original titles, but after a few years I stopped worrying about it. *Out on a Limb* and *Dangerous Beauty* have both been used before, several times, but none of the other books with those titles have content that is similar to mine. So readers aren't likely to get confused and buy the wrong book by mistake.

My *Dangerous Beauty* is a nonfiction book about bison and bears in Yellowstone. The other *Dangerous Beauty* books are fictional romances or thrillers. There are other *Out on a Limb* books in mysteries, but my cover and ethnic focus clearly differentiate it from the books with the same title. And the subtitle makes the distinction clear: *A Smoky Mountain Mystery*.

The increasingly large number of books being published every year will make it progressively harder to think up original titles, so subtitles and sub-genres will become more important.

The Worst Mistake
You Can Make

The worst mistake you can make with a title, subtitle and cover is to *not attract any readers at all.*

The second worst is to *attract the wrong readers*—people who, if they'd understood what your book was really about, or the tone it was actually written in, would never in a million years have bought your book.

These people, who are not professional book reviewers, will be annoyed by being misled and give your book a 1-star review. They'll say it's a *bad book*, that the writing is terrible, and the author is a deeply disturbed human being who should be taken off the street, and their parents should be sterilized so no more of these types of humans will come into being.

So your most important task after writing your book is to help the *right* potential readers self-select to buy your book and drive away all the others.

The Wonderful World of Sub-Genres and Micro-Niches

A couple of the bestselling genres are Mystery and Romance. Both of these genres have many sub-genres. Sub-genres are increasingly broken down further into very precise sub-categories.

One of the glories of Amazon is that while traditional brick and mortar bookstores didn't have enough shelf space to display a zillion genres—the online stores do. *Voila!* All the books that were previously ruled unpublishable by traditional presses because there was no designated category to shelve them in the Borders or B+N suddenly became viable.

The genres and sub-genres zone is an obscure area of Amazon you need to familiarize yourself with. You can tweak your manuscript to make it fit into a category where it can compete well. If you accidentally get your book in the wrong category it will die there.

It might take some work to figure out what the heck categories and sub-categories it should go in. This gets sorta complicated, but it's *crucial* to selling your book.

There are several separate category/genre trees on Amazon and you need to understand them all. There is ebook, print book, audio book. The print book tree is similar to what libraries use. The ebook tree is different. And the audio book tree is its own beast as well.

For example, if you look at the Medicine Men page at:
https://www.amazon.com/dp/B00A9L3E62/

The categories look like this:
#61 in Books > Medical Books > Medicine > Doctor-Patient Relations
#90 in Kindle Store > Kindle eBooks > Medical cBooks > Physician & Patient
#130 in Kindle Store > Kindle eBooks > Biographies & Memoirs > Professionals & Academics > Medical

Bear in the Back Seat 1 looks like this:
#5 in Kindle Store > Kindle eBooks > Nonfiction > Science > Biological Sciences > Animals > Bears
#12 in Books > Science & Math > Biological Sciences > Animals > Bears
#150 in Kindle Store > Kindle eBooks > Biographies & Memoirs > Travel

If you click on any of the categories or sub-categories you will see all the top books in that area. The page you're taken to has a left margin menu of all the categories and subcategories in that genre.

It looks like the left side of this page, for example:
https://www.amazon.com/gp/bestsellers/books/265542/

You can click forward or backward on those links and see how wide or how deep the individual genres and the sub-sub-genres go. It's a *lot* farther than a normal bookstore.

Attracting and Warning Potential Readers

This is just my way of handling things, but here goes: Some types of writing and some topics are what a very dear friend of mine would call a *special interest* reading. He means it's not for everyone.

Graphic violence (ubiquitous now, so I'm being an old maid here), especially lurid or salacious material (porn), detailed descriptions of body fluids, solids, and discharges of all types—just warn people. If you're writing unusually graphic or kinky or adult material of any kind be sure to use a cover, title, subtitle, and description of the book that telegraphs the content of your book. Or you will be very sorry.

You always want to make sure you attract the right readers and repel the wrong ones. This is *always* the main issue with *anyone's* material. Some people will love your style and others will hate it.

Whenever and whatever you write you wanna be sure to send up a flare to your best possible readers and toss a flash-bang grenade toward the people who could never possibly like a book like yours and who will give you a 1-star review for misleading them into thinking they might enjoy it.

This is why it makes sense for individual people to decide to write a book and publish it themselves.

Indie writers were thrilled to discover that if a writer could dominate even the tiniest micro-niche, they could make a good living with ebooks. Some writers make a fabulous high seven figure income in a micro-niche. For example, if you can reach nearly all of the book buyers in the world who are interested in mysteries solved by parrots, you'll be selling a lot of books.

Ebooks are extremely cheap to publish and the profit margin is much higher than for a traditionally published book. So these days, if you're selling ebooks well in a popular genre, you're getting rich.

People who are making millions on Amazon are in a wide range of genres, but these writers dominate their sub-category. They focus on writing a particular type of book and produce as many of them as they can in a series. Or multiple series(es).

Discounted Ebooks

If your book is traditionally published there will be constraints on how and what you are allowed to do to market your book. If you are traditionally published, the rest of the material in this section will be beyond your ability to personally participate in. The decision about whether any of the tactics below will be employed or not are totally within the purview of your publisher.

If you are independently publishing your book you will be able to control all the areas of your marketing, such as when and where your books are discounted, and how much they're discounted, and for how long, and where the discounted books are advertised.

This is a very important marketing technique, especially for ebooks.

Advertising Discounted Ebooks

Ebooks can be offered at the major vendors to be given away for free or sold for prices that have been discounted to any amount. The royalty percentage varies depending on the discounted price and across the various vendors.

This is a major, if not *the* most effective way to sell ebooks.

Temporarily Discounting an Ebook and Advertising It

One of the most important and cost-effective tactics for selling books these days is to discount it for a few days and advertise the discounted book by buying ads with various discounted ebook enewsletters like BookBub, KindleNationDaily, BargainBooksy EReaderNewsToday, and others.

There are many of these enewsletters and they each have their own targeted email lists designed to reach readers in various genres. The size of the mailing lists varies depending on which enewsletter service you're using and also by genre within each service.

You can discount an ebook to $2.99, $1.99, 99¢, or give it away for free. The most copies will go out if the book is free. The second most will go out at 99¢. The traditional publishing industry tends to keep their ebook discounts at $3.99-$1.99. Prices above 99¢ can severely limit the sales of the ebook unless it's particularly appealing.

Permanently Discounting an EBook and Advertising It

If your primary interest is getting your work out into the world, you can offer the ebook for free. Some authors will set the first book in a series free for the long term. The nickname for this is *perma-free.* The thinking is that if readers enjoy the first book for free, they'll buy the other books in the series. Free books that are appealing and professional looking can be given away at rates of tens of thousands a day if they are advertised well.

If I have a book that I think is a public service I'll offer it free periodically just because I think it will help people. For example I'll intermittently give away my book of vacation survival tips, *Waltzing With Wildlife: 10 Things NOT to Do in Our National Parks,* in the sincere hope of saving human and animals lives.

I gave away my first indie-published book, *Medicine Men,* because it had been turned down by 3 agents and 14 publishers. I wanted the information in the book out there in the world, but lost confidence that it was commercial until it went to #1 on Amazon and that massive exposure, and the wonderful reviews that came from the readers, jumpstarted my career.

It was a lucky accident that was motivated by hysteria over losing my job at age 58, having a stack of rejected manuscripts that I'd accumulated over the decade since the publication of my first book, and that I wanted the information in *Medicine Men* to get out there while the health care debate was raging nationwide.

Medicine Men was my way of putting my 2¢ worth into the national political debate on an issue that I cared about. And boy did I ever put it out there. Over 200,000 last time I looked. And I've made as much on that little indie book as I've made from my highly-regarded traditionally-published book. I've made more money with several of my indie books than I've made with my traditionally-published book.

Amazon Exclusively or Going Wide

You can offer an ebook for sale exclusively on Amazon in its KDP Select program. Amazon offers higher royalties in return for exclusivity and also some other aids to marketing

Many writers find that the lion's share of their sales are with Amazon so they decide to take the much easier route of selling exclusively there. The author interface at Amazon works better than the ones at other vendors. And the customer service is much better.

Some authors prefer to offer their work, especially ebooks, at multiple large online stores such as iTunes, B+N Nook, and Kobo. This requires different formatting (epub rather than mobi) and setting up author accounts at each vendor and learning to use each author interface.

Some authors make a significant portion of their income from these additional vendors. There are intelligent arguments supporting both strategies.

Audio Books

Amazon's audio division, ACX, also has exclusivity options that are more lucrative than offering your audio book through multiple audio vendors.

Print Books

For print books I use Amazon's CreateSpace. The author interface isn't too difficult for me to master and their customer service is pretty good. Every once in a while (especially around the rush season near Christmas) you'll get some damaged books sent out, but it's been very few indeed for me for the seven years I've been indie publishing. And they ship the replacements quickly to correct their mistakes.

I've never used any other printing service. There are others out there, for example Lightning Source, Lulu, and Ingram, but the various terms get complicated and so far I've been pleased with the results from CreateSpace. *(Not getting any kickbacks from The Zon as we call it for these recommendations of their services. The endorsement purely reflects my personal experience.)*

Writing a Pet Memoir
—Advice from Bob Tarte

The most important discovery I made when writing my first pet book, *Enslaved by Ducks*, is that the book wasn't just about the animals. It was about me and my relationship to them. Yes, the material centered on our bunnies—starting with belligerent Binky—then our aggressive little parrot Ollie, followed by an accidentally acquired first duck Daphne, and more and more critters after that. But I was never absent from the story. In fact, it's no exaggeration to say that I figured into every single word, because I was the person writing every single word.

You can't write a book about a pet without also focusing on you, the pet owner, because, by definition, a pet is an animal that someone 'owns' or 'keeps' as a companion—or, in my case, is enslaved by in rewarding and vexing ways. This is by no means a bad thing, so don't go thinking, "Ugh. I want to write about my boa constrictor, Sir Squeeze-a-Lot. Not about me." Writing about yourself creates the framework for talking about your pets and adds depth and entertainment to your tale.

I didn't understand this when I first started writing *Enslaved by Ducks*, envisioning it very differently than how it ended up. I thought it would be fun to write chapters about traits shared by different pets rather than telling a larger and more-or-less chronological story. I even had a different title in mind. *All Our Pets are Pests.*

My first chapter of *All Our Pets are Pest* focused on pet projects—obsessive activities or projects undertaken by our critters. In that opening chapter I described how, as soon as we let him out of his cage, our rabbit Binky made a beeline for our bedroom and wiggled behind the headboard, where we couldn't reach him. He loved to drive us nuts. We plugged the crack between the wall and the headboard with pillows. Once he became adept at pillow removal, we blocked his access to his hidey-hole with suitcases. He just wouldn't quit. Instead of enjoying his freedom roaming around the house, Binky was fixated on getting behind the bed.

In that same chapter, I described our African grey parrot Stanley Sue and her secret woodwork project. To all appearances, during her out-of-cage hours, she stood on top of Binky's cage in the dining room chewing on cardboard from record LP mailers, which gave our dining room that special decorator's touch. Little did we realize that the cardboard was just a front. When we weren't in the room, Stanley Sue reached around behind the cardboard mailers and chewed up our woodwork as effectively as a colony of termites.

Chapter two was to center on the theme of animal escape artists. I would describe how Binky never met an outdoor pen that he couldn't find his way out of, and also how our little parrot Ollie somehow managed to get out of the house twice. Luckily, his wings were clipped and he couldn't fly away.

I gave up in the middle of writing this chapter. The book just wasn't coming together the way I wanted it to. I had a string of disconnected incidents rather than a story, and the full personalities of our animals failed to shine through. My relationship to the animals wasn't explained well, either. Did I love them? Did I hate them? Or were they simply research subjects?

Focusing on my relationship to our pets turned out to be the key. I tossed out what I had written and started over, ultimately (after some further thrashing around) taking a more traditional approach of telling the story of each pet, beginning with how my wife Linda and I got them and how they fit into our lives. Before long, I understood what *Enslaved by Ducks* was really about. It was the story of how a person who never cared a bit about animals—that would be me—ended up falling in love with them and serving their every whim.

My editor at Algonquin Books of Chapel Hill, Kathy Pories, came up with the brilliant subtitle that perfectly summed up the book. *How One Man Went from Head of the Household to Bottom of the Pecking Order.*

The result was a book that continues to sell since it first came out in hardcover in 2003. The Kindle version made the Wall Street Journal bestsellers list and was the number one bestselling pet book on Amazon at that time.

The success doesn't end there. Currently, *Enslaved by Ducks* has been optioned for adaptation as a feature film. This may or may not happen, but it's exciting either way.

Thank you, enslaving pets!

Now here's the important part. If I can write a book, you can write a book. You don't have to quit your job, wall yourself into your secret writing room, and dedicate yourself to a monastic existence. You don't have to be particularly brilliant, positive minded, or ambitious, either. I'm not any of those things. All you have to do is stick with the writing, even if you can only spend an hour a day, and half of that time is devoted to staring out the window. Some days I'm happy to write a single paragraph. Like this one! Okay, better than this one, but not by all that much.

Fine-tuning Your Narrative Voice

All four of my pet memoirs are unmistakably written by the same person, and yet the voice is different in each one. These differences might not be obvious, and that's a good thing, since you don't want to call too much attention to the voice. It should be there but not there, an invisible guide that takes your readers by the elbow and steers them through the story.

It isn't as if I have a vast amount of room for movement in terms of tweaking my narrative voice, since I'm not particularly flexible when it comes to the way I view the world. Still, I was eventually able to fall into the right voice based on the stories I had decided to tell and the idea behind each book.

I decided to write *Enslaved by Ducks* after reading Bill Bryson's *A Walk in the Woods*, a hilarious story about his attempt to walk the Appalachian Trail with his misfit friend Katz. It excited me the way he made the most mundane parts of his journey funny, so I challenged myself to try to write a book about our pets in which every single sentence carried a humorous observation or an unexpected twist.

I wasn't able to do that exactly. But *Enslaved by Duck* is filled with my wonder over the behavior of our pet ducks, geese, bunnies, parrots, parakeets, a dove, and a cat. They amazed and befuddled me. They were experts at manipulating my wife and me into getting what they wanted, and my own duck-out-of-water personality as I dealt with these strange beings formed the voice of the book. That point of view came naturally as I reported on events, but I shoved it forward by trying to achieve my goal of making the telling constantly funny. Some readers got it. Others didn't, complaining that the author was too whiny and self-centered, and what a wimp he was for always caving into his wife's desires for yet another animal. But you can't please everybody, and I managed to please enough people to make the book a success.

As I was finishing writing *Enslaved by Ducks*, my life turned difficult. My father, a perpetually healthy, unflappable man who acted and looked fifteen years younger than his age of eighty-four, died of a heart attack while shoveling snow. My mom's memory problems abruptly worsened, and all at once she was no longer in stolid command of her life and emotions. Around our house, we lost some of our pets, including one of my dearest, my African grey parrot Stanley Sue.

I didn't know how to write about any of this at first. Then I thought about trying to push the boundaries of the type of stories usually included in a pet book. So I let the chaos of life leak into the pages, telling a sad story in a largely humorous vein, taking a laughter-through-tears approach, which I thought was kind of brave. But my amazement over the turns that events had taken in *Enslaved by Ducks* had become a tone of shock in *Fowl Weather*. Readers expecting more fluffy stories about a city boy's poor adjustment to rural life weren't prepared for the darker tone in the follow-up. I think the voice was well suited to the material. Less jokey, more introspective, sharper, occasionally plumbing depths seldom found in humor writing. But *Fowl Weather* wasn't a commercial success, and I didn't know where to go next.

One day it struck me that somehow, without meaning to, we had ended up with six cats, and each of them had a story to tell. And I had a story of my own about sharing a small house with them. "You can't even sit on the toilet without a cat staring at you," Linda complained, and I was off and running with *Kitty Cornered*. I decided to avoid the complexity of *Fowl Weather* and its steady stream of misfortune in favor of the straightforward chronicle of how each cat came to us, focusing on their annoying but endearing quirks and the brightness they ultimately brought into our lives. I kept the cats at the center of the narrative rather than spotlighting my neuroses. At least I thought I had. But a few one-star reviews on Amazon again complained about the author's whining, and a glowing five-star review praised the book as the "self-portrait of a man who exists in more or less constant psychic pain." The book sold well enough that it earned back my advance from the publisher— so who am I to whine about having a whiny narrative voice?

I had to make a change for *Feather Brained*, however. For the first time ever, I was writing a book that contained factual content that could be argued with if I made glaring errors. The subject was wild birds and how I learned to find and identify them. While I didn't intend to present myself as a bird authority, and couldn't have carried off the impersonation if I had wanted to, I need to establish a dram of credibility for my story to have any weight. The "I" had to be a narrator who knew something about birds looking back in forbearing derision at the author's pre-birding days of frightened, city-bred cluelessness in a forest, meadow, or woodlot.

Nearly every chapter of *Feather Brained* includes a meeting or conversation with a genuine birding expert, and I could hardly blend their contributions into the exact same clownish atmosphere that lit and/or dragged down my other books. Therefore I tempered my neurotic excesses, toned down the exaggeration from a nine to a seven, and kept the focus on my love of birds. The book is also the love story of my marriage to Linda, who first introduced me to the not-so-terrible joys of rural life, and I was happy that so many readers picked up on the romantic theme.

To my ears, the voice is different in each of my books. I made a conscious effort to make it different in order to suit the material. No reader has grumbled that I didn't sound in one book like I sounded in another, so I consider my voice tweaking to be transparent and successful. I can't do much about that whining, though.

About Reviews

I write humorous books about animals. Pet ducks, geese, cats, bunnies, parrots, and wild birds. And I get hate mail. I receive unhinged comments on Amazon, too. I don't receive a lot of this stuff, but any amount of hate is too much hate, especially when all I'm doing is describing our lives with animals.

Most of the comments from readers of *Enslaved By Ducks, Fowl Weather,* and *Kitty Cornered* josh me about spoiling our animals, and deservedly so. My wife Linda used to sing a lullaby to our grumpy rabbit Binky. And we once kept a goose named Liza on our front porch for an entire summer while nursing her through a lung infection—plying her with bowls of duck pellets, dandelion greens, water, and gourmet-quality mud.

So I'm surprised when I'm occasionally scolded for not lavishing enough care upon our pampered critters. And a few times, I've been accused of outright animal abuse.

"You People Make Me Sick"

Our first bunny, Binky died from an unknown malady after acting listless for a few days. Linda rushed him to the vet when he suddenly grew worse. We hadn't realized that once a bunny shows signs of illness, it is often too late to help. We had read books on keeping rabbits, phoned the breeder frequently for help, and did our best for him. But this was in the pre-Internet era when life's mysteries were further than a Google search away.

Maybe I should have included a disclaimer to this effect. A reader responded to Binky's story in *Enslaved By Ducks* by snail-mailing me a sheet on basic rabbit care adorned with a sticky-note that said, "You people make me sick."

The same book contains the story of Weaver, a starling we rescued who was unable to fly. We had just started raising and releasing orphaned songbirds for Wildlife Rehab Center in Grand Rapids, and Linda successfully brought Weaver and his siblings to a state of ear-splitting good health.

She fed them the standard-recipe formula that rehabbers use with insectivorous birds: kitten kibbles, pureed chicken baby food, a squirt of liquid vitamins, and water, all slushed together in a blender. Weaver eventually took wing and left us. But a reader emailed me, outraged and frothing at the keyboard that we had fed him such a concoction. "I would bring charges against you if I could," she wrote.

Because of comments like these—as well as an online review criticizing *Enslaved By Ducks* as the worst conceivable 'how-to' book, though I had written it as a 'how-not-to' book— I find myself over-explaining things these days rather than assuming that readers will realize we're not secretly running a taxidermy service. And I never post photos of our duck and goose quarters on Facebook or Twitter or show our indoor birds cavorting loose in the dining room. But there's a stronger reason for being cautious than staving off criticism from the occasional malcontent. I want to decrease the odds of my contributing to anyone's animal mishap.

Here's an example of what I mean. I wrote a book about our six cats called *Kitty Cornered*. My sister Joan and her husband Jack with their twelve cats made several appearances, beginning with Jack live-trapping three feral cats with the help of a wireless video camera and the hindrance of many sleepless nights. Once the cats were settled on the front porch, and after one of the females unexpectedly had kittens, Joan and Jack took them successively to the vet to get them spayed or neutered. Before releasing them into the house to mingle with Winston, Gizmo, Mimi, Linus, Libby Lou, and Max, they also had them tested for feline leukemia.

I mentioned these tests more than once in *Kitty Cornered*, but not because it contributed to my madcap narrative. I included it because I didn't want a single reader to introduce a feline leukemia-positive kitty into their home and endanger their other cats due to information that I failed to include.

Some details, however, are probably best excluded from a pet book. In *Fowl Weather* I chronicled a horrendous July in which five of our animals died, including a Muscovy duck who somehow managed to hang himself in the fencing while trying to get at a rival in an adjacent pen, and in a different pen on the opposite end of our property, two khaki Campbell ducks that fell victim to a burrowing raccoon.

A reader chided me for being reckless about housing our animals, and he was probably right in the case of the industrious raccoon. But he was reaching when it came to the unfortunate Muscovy who only managed to hang himself through a bizarre series of circumstances that had never remotely occurred to us as possible. Nevertheless, we immediately took steps to make sure it couldn't happen again. But despite what some of readers want to believer, it's impossible to plan for everything.

It's Hopeless, So Just Give Up

In the end, you can write and write and write, but people will still read into your book whatever they want to. An Amazon customer reviewing *Enslaved by Ducks* complained, "The author and his wife are poster children for irresponsible animal care. Do no research, see no vet, allow inappropriate and unsafe living and behavior, and think it's funny." I almost always ignore negative comments online, but once in a while when a reader makes a statement that is totally dishonest, I feel obligated to respond.

"If Bob and Linda 'see no vet,' then why are there seven veterinarians listed in the Cast of Characters?" I asked. "And if they 'allow inappropriate and unsafe living and behavior,' then why do licensed animal rehabbers bring them animals to care for?"

Sometimes even positive comments veer off into the surreal. At the beginning of *Fowl Weather* I included a Cast of Characters, because our many animals (36 at the time) were hard for readers to keep track of. I grouped the cast under three headings: 'Nonhuman' for animals, 'Humans' for us lesser beings, and 'Inhumans' for entities like the telephone that have power over our lives. Just for a gag, I put my friend Bill Holm in the 'Nonhuman' category to emphasize his standing as an annoyance.

A book reviewer for a North Carolina newspaper was generous in her positive comments about *Fowl Weather*. And she chuckled about the scenes that featured my "imaginary friend Bill Holm." Being imaginary came as quite a bombshell to the real-life Bill Holm, who insists that he exists.

That critic accurately recounted all other facts about *Fowl Weather* in her review, unlike another who groused that she found it impossible to finish the book because of its supposed prejudice against the elderly. Ignoring the fact that I'm hardly in the bloom of youth myself, the comment is breathtaking considering that a major thread of the memoir was my mom's fight with Alzheimer's disease and my family's efforts to help her.

A few years ago, Linda ran an ad in our local paper seeking help with a strenuous landscaping job. One man who applied had an obvious physical impairment that made it difficult for us to imagine how he could perform the work.

When I wrote about the incident in *Fowl Weather*, I didn't want readers in our community to say, "Oh my, gosh, that's so-and-so," so I disguised the man by making him asthmatic rather than describing his condition. That critic who accused me of age discrimination decided that my passage about the asthmatic was more evidence of my grudge against the elderly, even though the age of the fellow was never indicated. I should have noted in *Fowl Weather* that he was in his forties, and I should have taken pains to emphasize Bill Holm's corporeality, too.

Unbearable Recklessness

This brings me back to the reader who posted the online comment that we lost some of our animals due to substandard housing. One afternoon in early spring, Linda took a walk through the woods behind our house. Spotting what she thought was a crow's nest in a tree, she focused her binoculars and backed slowly away after realizing that the big brown heap was, in fact, a bear.

I didn't believe her at first. We're way too far south in Michigan for bears, but I saw the sleeping animal myself and backed away at a speedier clip than she had. But what if the bear had come crashing through the woods to tear apart our backyard poultry pen as if it had been made of matchsticks? What potential havoc might someone's escaped pet mountain lion wreak on the outdoor pets? Shouldn't we anticipate every single potential threat and act accordingly?

I'm afraid I can't answer these questions. I'm too busy at the moment. I've started work on a rooftop meteor deflection screen to protect our parrots on the first floor, and I'll definitely include the plans in the appendix of my next book. I just hope I'm not overdoing the over-explaining. It's humorous animal books I write, after all.

Bob Tarte's latest memoir is *Feather Brained—My Bumbling Quest to Become a Birder and Find a Rare Bird on My Own,* published by University of Michigan Press. He is also the author of the pet memoirs *Enslaved by Ducks, Fowl Weather,* and *Kitty Cornered,* all published by Algonquin Books of Chapel Hill.

Acknowledgments

This book would not have been possible without the Facebook Group:
https://www.facebook.com/groups/memoirists/

I'd especially like to thank—

Bob Tarte
George Hodgman
Mark Garrison
Jeremy Blachman
Mary Ann Fry
Cayr Ariel Wulff

Jack Degerlia

Kate Belt
Betty Newman
Jill Draper
Katrina Waltenbaugh
Tiffany Young

About Carolyn Jourdan

USA Today, Audible, and 5-Time Wall Street Journal best-selling author of heartwarming memoir, biography, and mystery - Jourdan chronicles miracles, mayhem, and madcap moments in Appalachian medicine, as well as zany and touching interactions with wildlife in the Great Smoky Mountains National Park.

Jourdan's trademark blend of wit and wisdom, humor and humanity have earned her high praise from Dolly Parton and Fannie Flagg, as well as major national newspapers, the New York Public Library, Elle, Family Circle Magazine, and put her work at the top of hundreds of lists of best books of the year and funniest books ever.

Carolyn is a former U.S. Senate Counsel to the Committee on Environment and Public Works and the Committee on Governmental Affairs. She has degrees from the University of Tennessee in Biomedical Engineering and Law. She lives on the family farm in Strawberry Plains, Tennessee, with many stray animals.

Visit her at www.CarolynJourdan.com and hear her read stories from her books.

http://facebook.com/CarolynJourdan
http://facebook.com/CarolynJourdanAuthor
http://twitter.com/CarolynJourdan

Printed in Great Britain
by Amazon